AVENGING SPIDER-MAN

MY FRIENDS CAN BEAT UP YOUR FRIENDS

WRITER
ZEB WELLS

#1-3

ARTIST
JOE MADUREIRA

COLOR ARTIST
DOMMO AYMARA

COVER ART
JOE MADUREIRA WITH **ARON LUSEN** (#1)
& **FERRAN DANIEL** (#2-3)

#4

PENCILER
GREG LAND

INKER
JAY LEISTEN

COLORIST
WIL QUINTANA

COVER ART
GREG LAND WITH **JUSTIN PONSOR**

PENCILER
LEINIL FRANCIS YU

OLORIST
UNNY GHO

COVER ART
LEINIL FRANCIS YU WITH **JASON KEITH**

LETTERER: VC'S JOE CARAMAGNA ASSISTANT EDITOR: ELLIE PYLE

ASSOCIATE EDITOR: ALEJANDRO ARBONA EDITOR: STEPHEN WACKER

EXECUTIVE EDITOR: TOM BREVOORT

Collection Editor: Jennifer Grünwald • Assistant Editors: Alex Starbuck & Nelson Ribeiro • Editor, Special Projects: Mark D. Beazley
Senior Editor, Special Projects: Jeff Youngquist • Senior Vice President of Sales: David Gabriel
SVP of Brand Planning & Communications: Michael Pasciullo • Book Design: Jeff Powell

Editor in Chief: Axel Alonso • Chief Creative Officer: Joe Quesada • Publisher: Dan Buckley • Executive Producer: Alan Fine

VENGING SPIDER-MAN: MY FRIENDS CAN BEAT UP YOUR FRIENDS. Contains material originally published in magazine form as AVENGING SPIDER-MAN #1-5. First printing 2012. Hardcover ISBN# 978-0 Softcover ISBN# 978-0-7851-5779-3. Published by MARVEL WORLDWIDE, INC., a subsidiary of MARVEL ENTERTAINMENT, LLC. OFFICE OF PUBLICATION: 135 West 50th Street, New York, NY 10020. Copyright © arvel Characters, Inc. All rights reserved. Hardcover: $24.99 per copy in the U.S. and $27.99 in Canada (GST #R127032852). Softcover: $19.99 per copy in the U.S. and $21.99 in Canada (GST #R127 greement #40668537. All characters featured in this issue and the distinctive names and likenesses thereof, and all related indicia are trademarks of Marvel Characters, Inc. No similarity between any of th ersons, and/or institutions in this magazine with those of any living or dead person or institution is intended, and any such similarity which may exist is purely coincidental. **Printed in the U.S.A.** ALAN F resident, Marvel Worldwide, Inc. and EVP & CMO Marvel Characters B.V.; DAN BUCKLEY, Publisher & President - Print, Animation & Digital Divisions; JOE QUESADA, Chief Creative Officer; TOM BREVOORT OGART, SVP of Operations & Procurement, Publishing; RUWAN JAYATILLEKE, SVP & Associate Publisher, Publishing; C.B. CEBULSKI, SVP of Creator & Content Development; DAVID GABRIEL, SVP of ICHAEL PASCIULLO, SVP of Brand Planning & Communications; JIM O'KEEFE, VP of Operations & Logistics; DAN CARR, Executive Director of Publishing Technology; SUSAN CRESPI, Editorial Oper ublishing Operations Manager; STAN LEE, Chairman Emeritus. For information regarding advertising in Marvel Comics or on Marvel.com, please contact John Dokes, SVP Integrated Sales a om. For Marvel subscription inquiries, please call 800-217-9158. **Manufactured between 4/30/2012 and 5/28/2012 (hardcover), and 4/30/2012 and 10/1/2012 (softcover), by R.R. DONK**

987654321

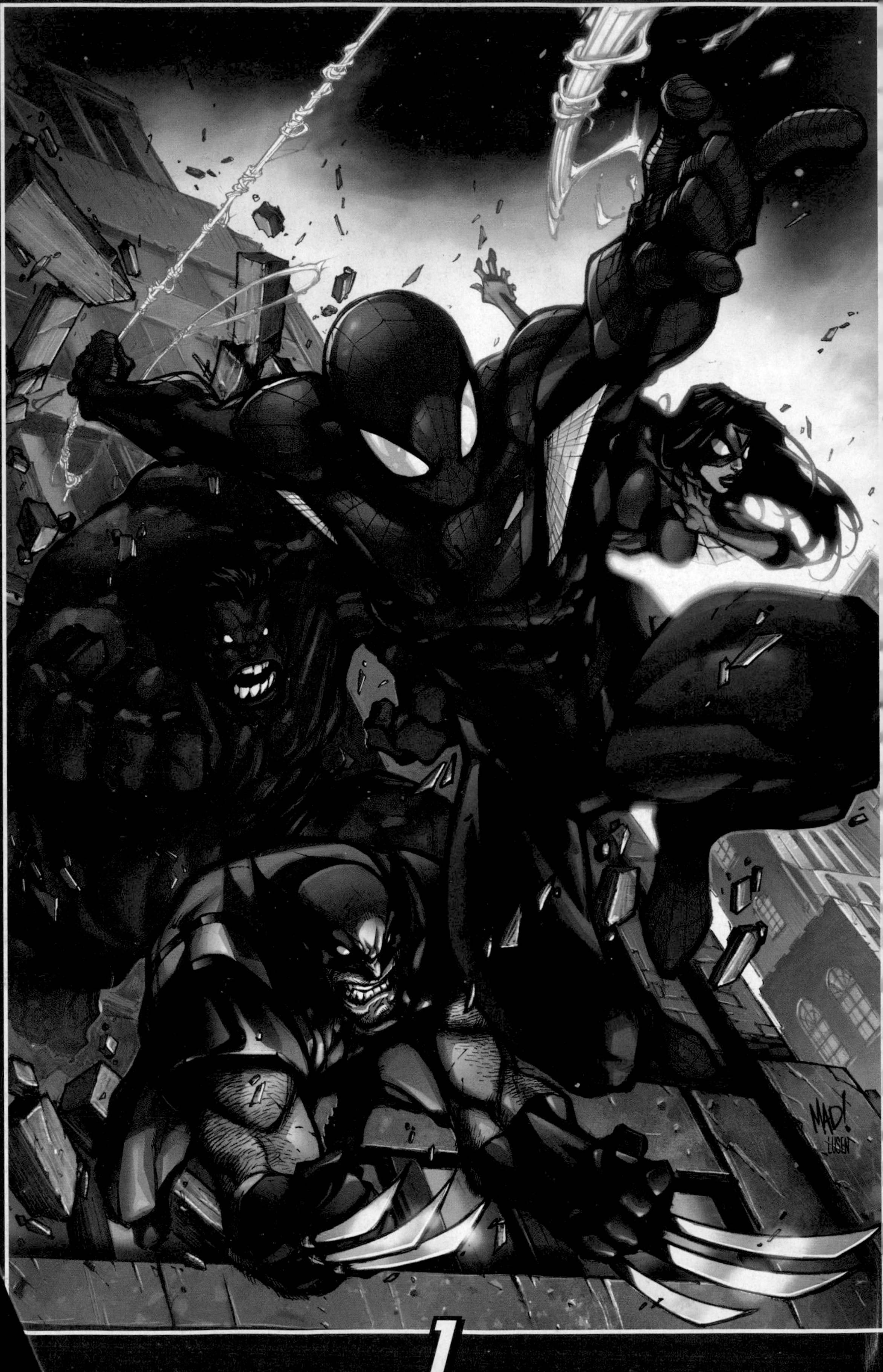
MAD!
LUSEN

1

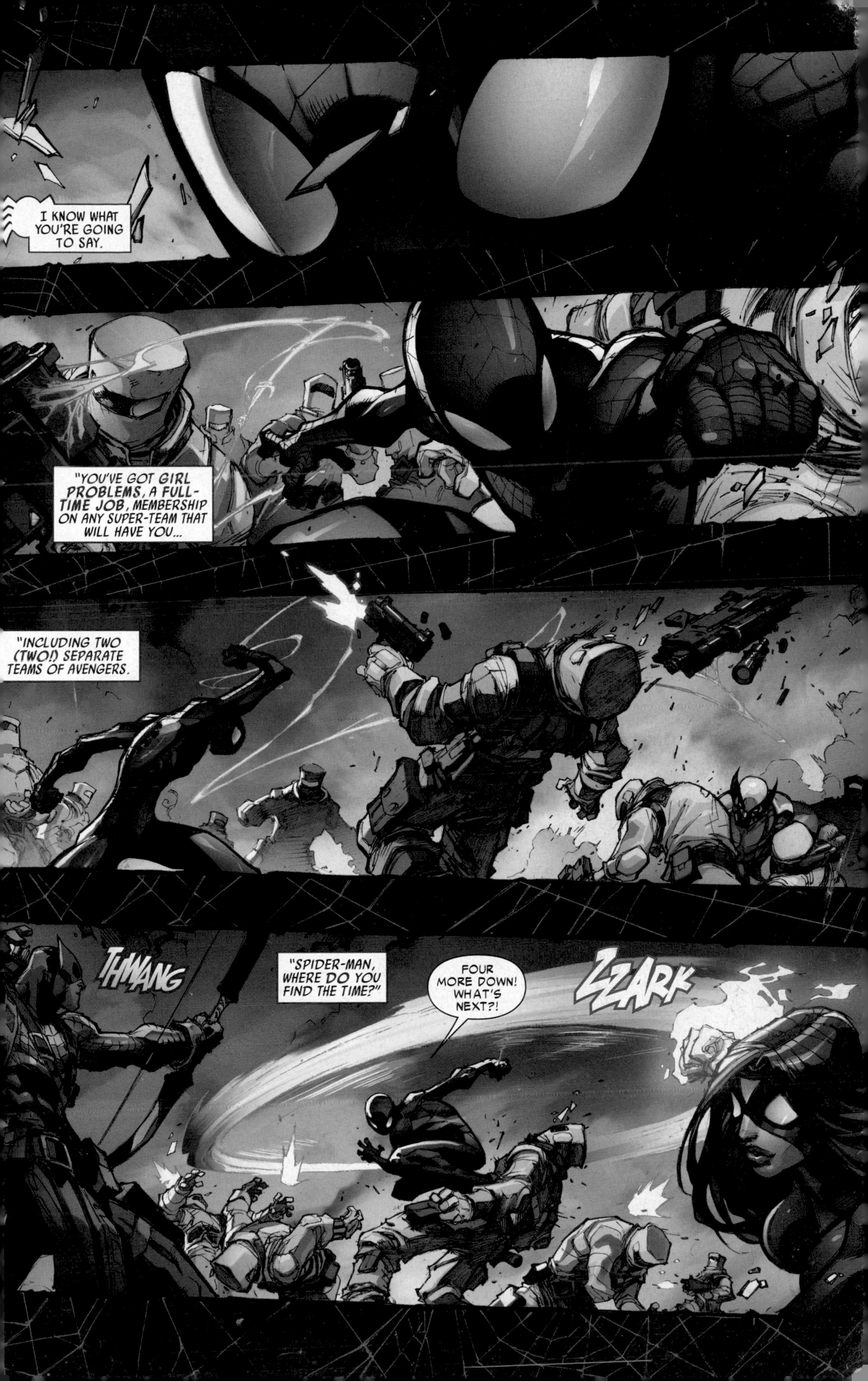
I KNOW WHAT YOU'RE GOING TO SAY.
"YOU'VE GOT GIRL PROBLEMS, A FULL-TIME JOB, MEMBERSHIP ON ANY SUPER-TEAM THAT WILL HAVE YOU...
"INCLUDING TWO (TWO!) SEPARATE TEAMS OF AVENGERS.
THWANG
"SPIDER-MAN, WHERE DO YOU FIND THE TIME?"
FOUR MORE DOWN! WHAT'S NEXT?!
ZZARK

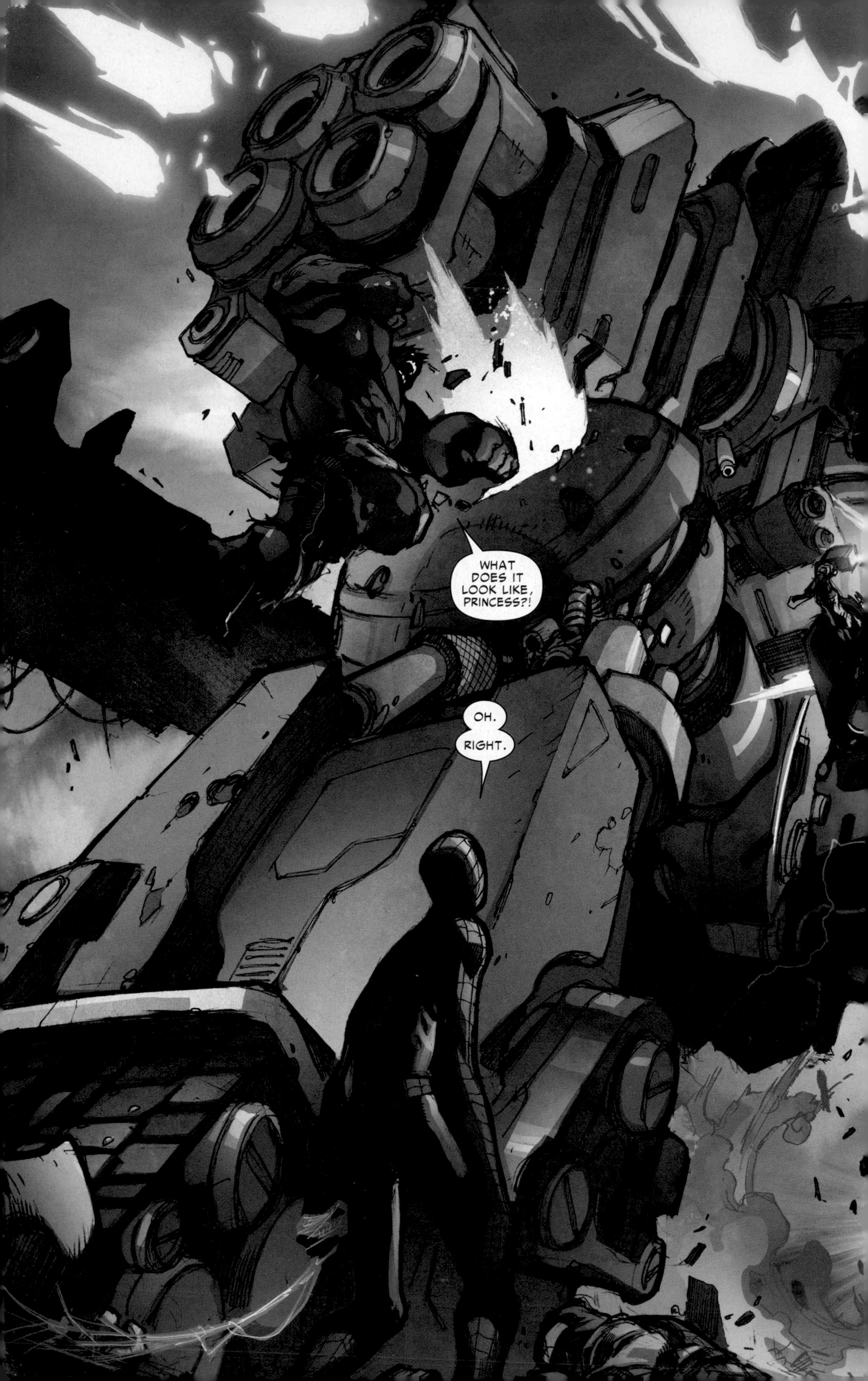
WHAT DOES IT LOOK LIKE, PRINCESS?!
OH.
RIGHT.

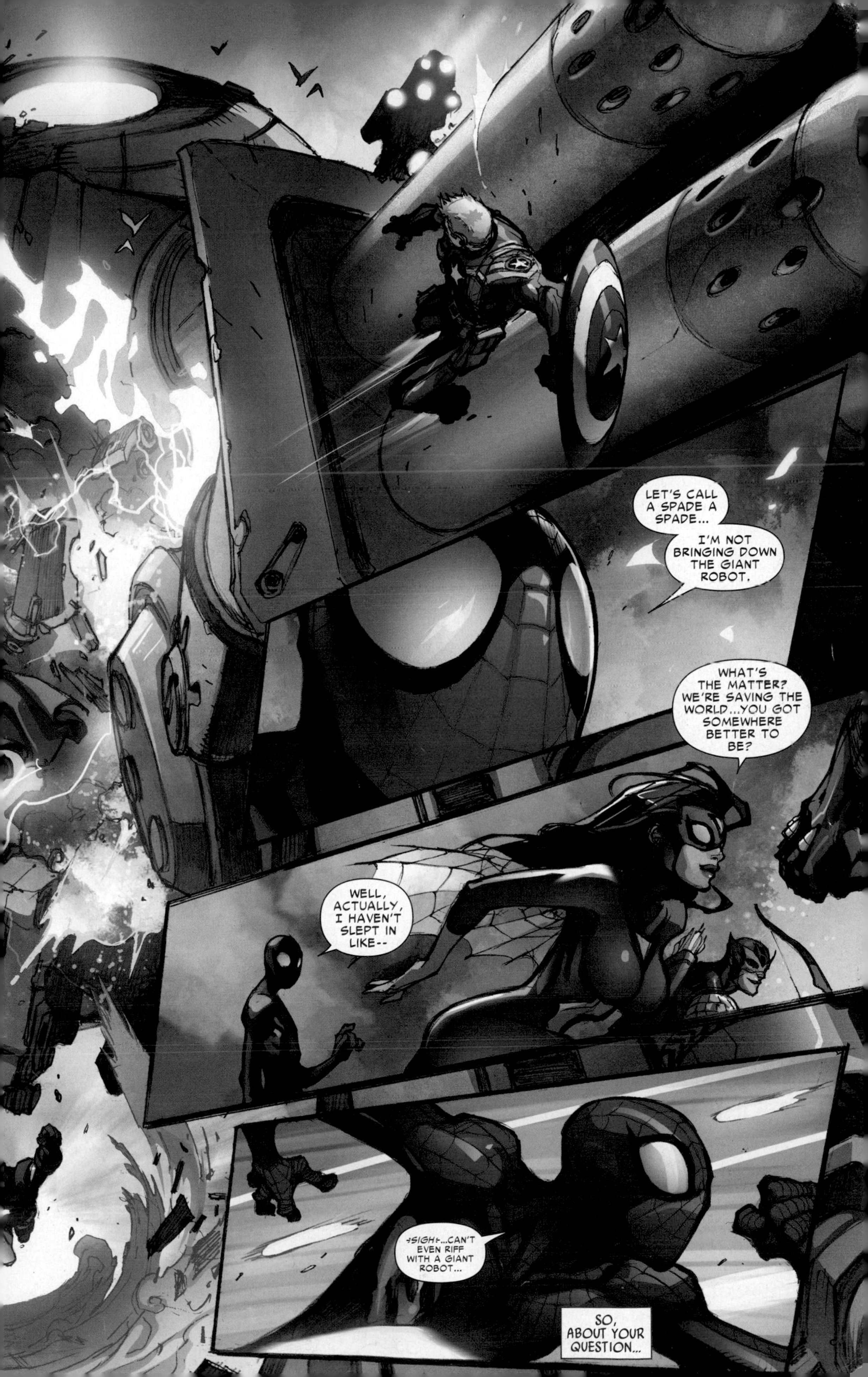

LET'S CALL A SPADE A SPADE...
I'M NOT BRINGING DOWN THE GIANT ROBOT.
WHAT'S THE MATTER? WE'RE SAVING THE WORLD...YOU GOT SOMEWHERE BETTER TO BE?
WELL, ACTUALLY, I HAVEN'T SLEPT IN LIKE--
SIGH...CAN'T EVEN RIFF WITH A GIANT ROBOT...
SO, ABOUT YOUR QUESTION...

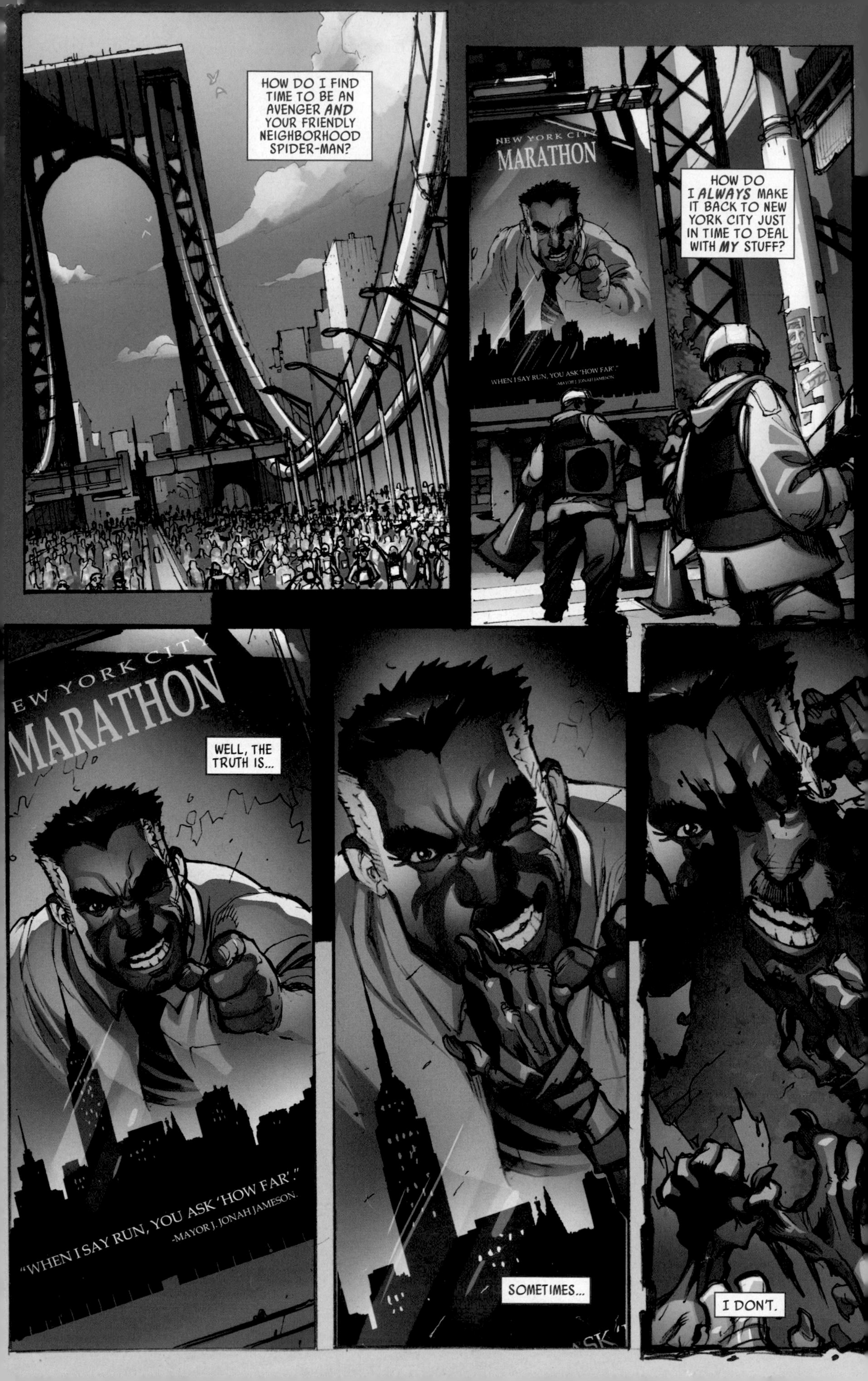
HOW DO I FIND TIME TO BE AN AVENGER AND YOUR FRIENDLY NEIGHBORHOOD SPIDER-MAN?
NEW YORK CITY
MARATHON
WHEN I SAY RUN, YOU ASK "HOW FAR."
-MAYOR J. JONAH JAMESON
HOW DO I ALWAYS MAKE IT BACK TO NEW YORK CITY JUST IN TIME TO DEAL WITH MY STUFF?
EW YORK CITY
MARATHON
WELL, THE TRUTH IS...
"WHEN I SAY RUN, YOU ASK 'HOW FAR'."
-MAYOR J. JONAH JAMESON.
SOMETIMES...
I DON'T.

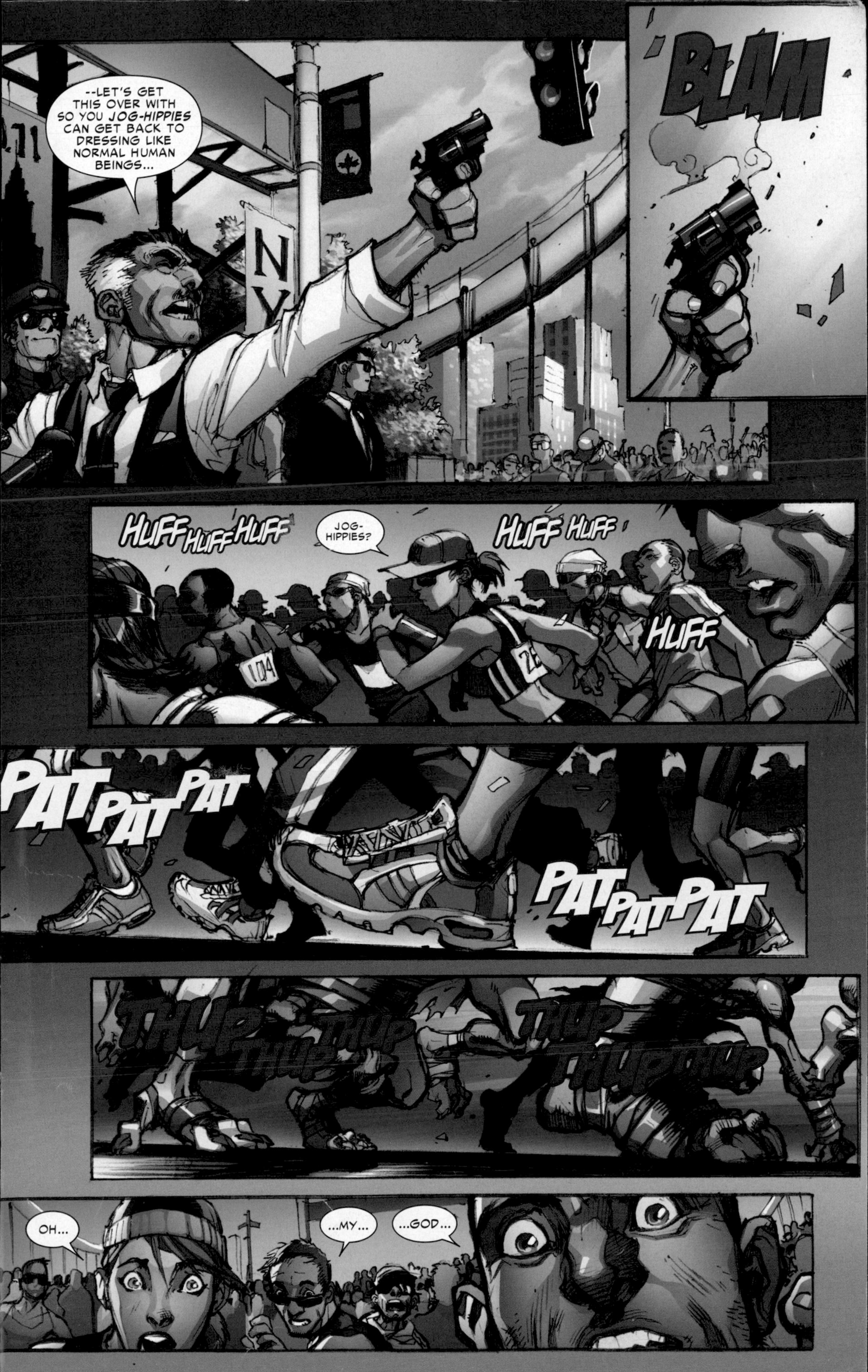
--LET'S GET THIS OVER WITH SO YOU JOG-HIPPIES CAN GET BACK TO DRESSING LIKE NORMAL HUMAN BEINGS...
NY
BLAM
HUFF HUFF HUFF
JOG-HIPPIES?
HUFF HUFF
HUFF
PAT PAT PAT
PAT PAT PAT
THUP THUP THUP
THUP THUP THUP
OH...
...MY...
...GOD...

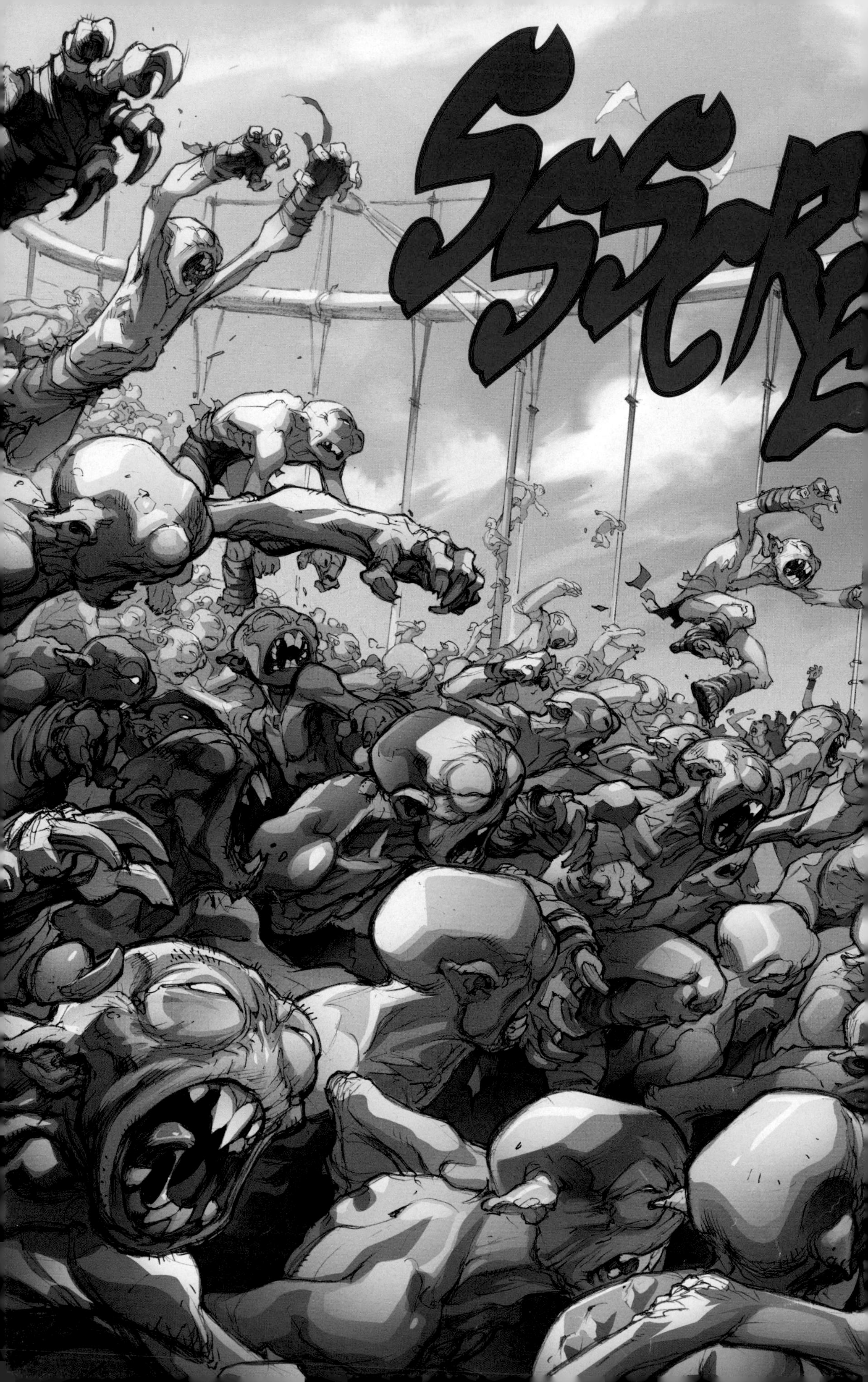
SSSCRE

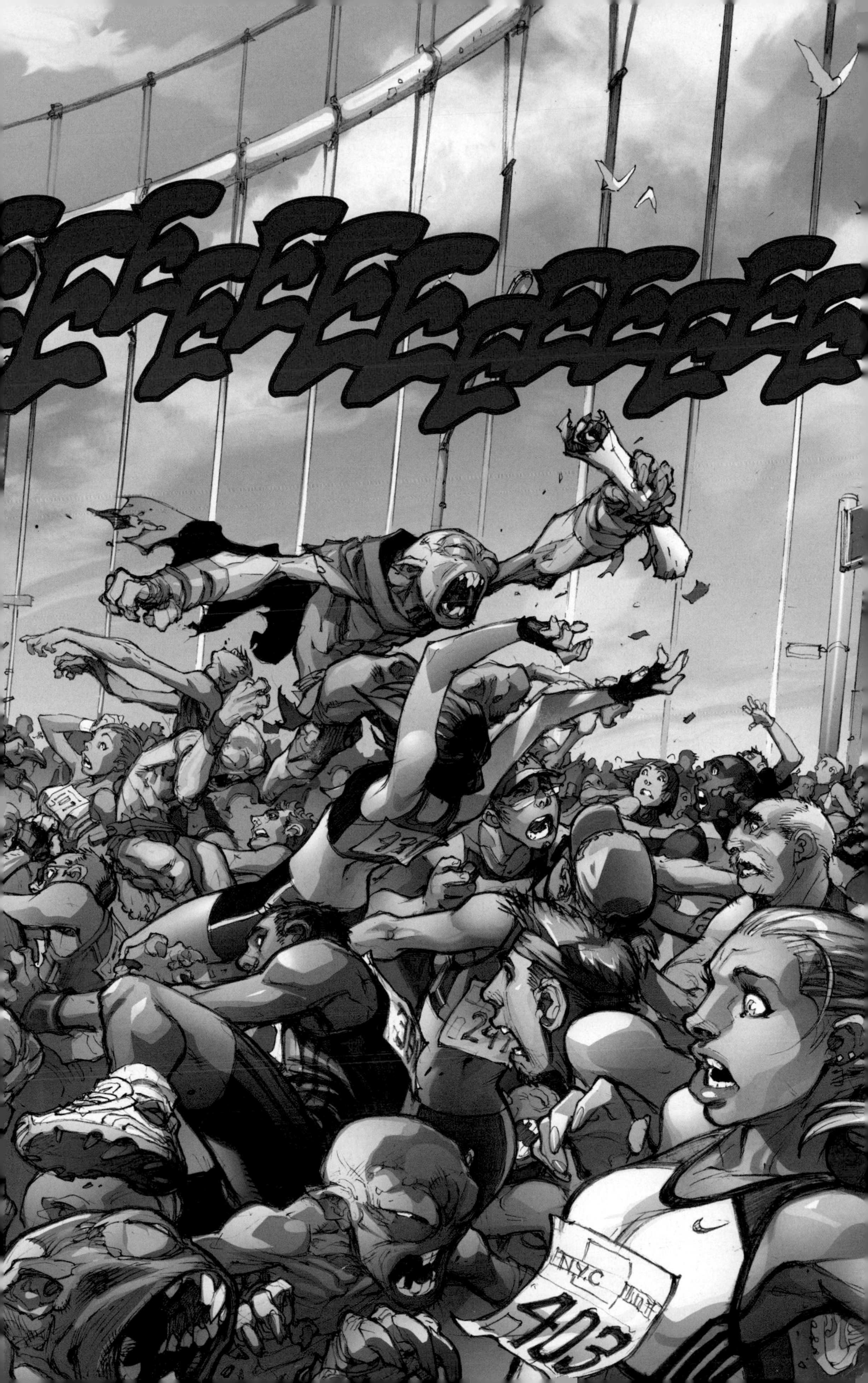

EEEEEEEEEEEEEE
N.Y.C
403

While attending a demonstration in radiology, high school student Peter Parker was bitten by a spider which had accidentally been exposed to radioactive rays. Through a miracle of science, Peter soon found that he had gained the spider's powers... and had, in effect, become a human spider! From that day on he was the...

AVENGING SPIDER-MAN

AVEN
SPIDE

WRITER: ZEB WELLS

COLOR ART: FERRAN DANIEL

PRODUCTION ASSIST: **MANNY MEDEROS**   ASSISTANT EDITOR: **ELLIE PYLE**

EDITOR IN CHIEF: **AXEL ALONSO**   CHIEF CREATIVE OFFICER: **JOE QUESADA**

VARIANT COVER ARTISTS: **RAMOS & DELGADO; CAMPBELL & DE**

BLANK VARIANT BY

General Thaddeus "Thunderbolt" Ross was a decorated war hero who fiercely hunted the Hulk. After several futile years of chasing the original Green Goliath, Ross sought vengeance and made a pact for power with the evil Intelegencia. Imbued with the powers of super-strength, energy absorption and gamma radiation... he now seeks redemption as...

GING
R-MAN

ARTIST: **JOE MADUREIRA**

LETTERER: **VC's JOE CARAMAGNA**

EDITOR: **STEPHEN WACKER**   EXECUTIVE EDITOR: **TOM BREVOORT**

PUBLISHER: **DAN BUCKLEY**   EXECUTIVE PRODUCER: **ALAN FINE**

JOE QUESADA, DANNY MIKI, & RICHARD ISANOVE

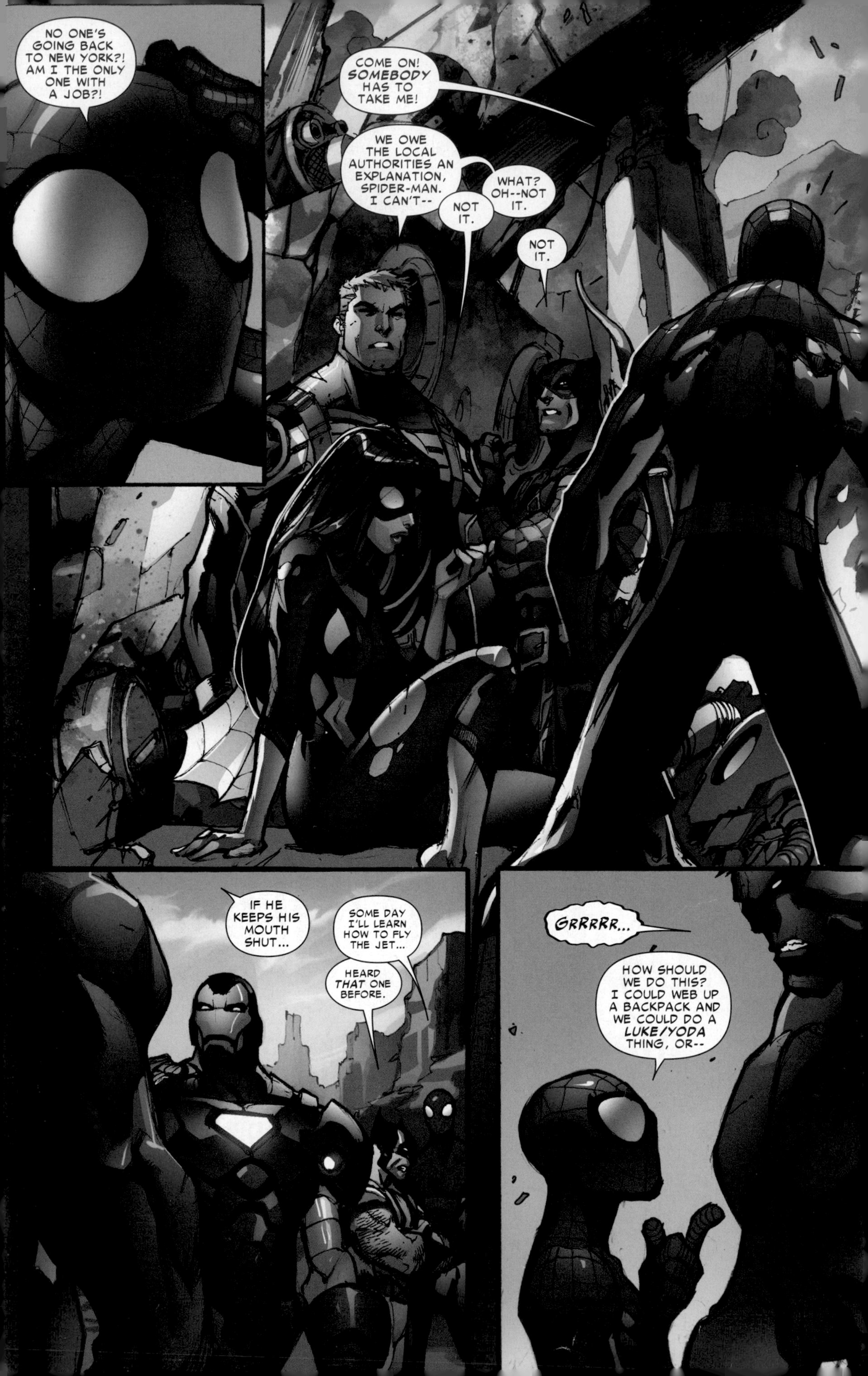
NO ONE'S GOING BACK TO NEW YORK?! AM I THE ONLY ONE WITH A JOB?!
COME ON! SOMEBODY HAS TO TAKE ME!
WE OWE THE LOCAL AUTHORITIES AN EXPLANATION, SPIDER-MAN. I CAN'T--
NOT IT.
WHAT? OH--NOT IT.
NOT IT.
IF HE KEEPS HIS MOUTH SHUT...
SOME DAY I'LL LEARN HOW TO FLY THE JET...
HEARD THAT ONE BEFORE.
GRRRRR...
HOW SHOULD WE DO THIS? I COULD WEB UP A BACKPACK AND WE COULD DO A LUKE/YODA THING, OR--

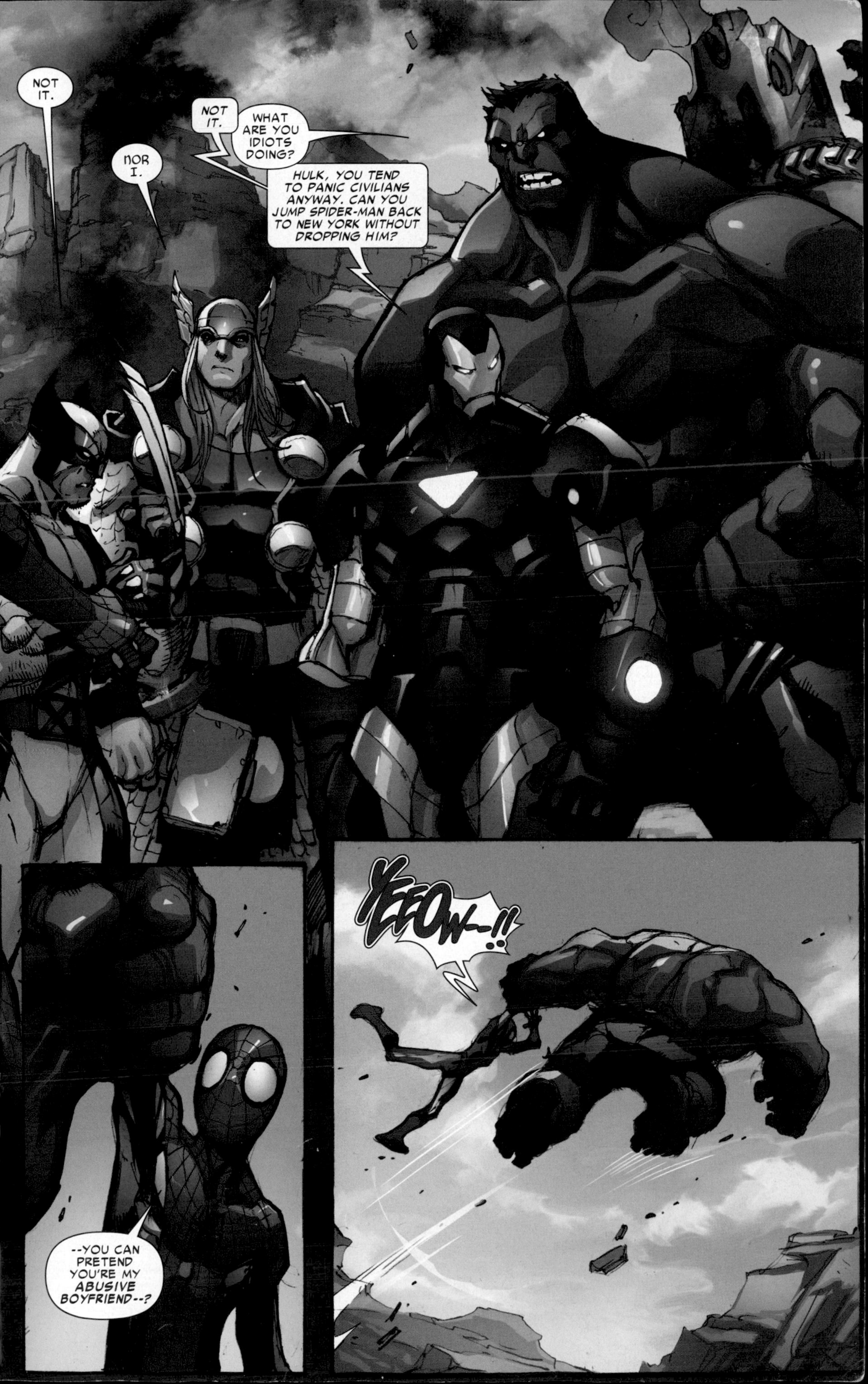
NOT IT.
NOT IT.
WHAT ARE YOU IDIOTS DOING?
NOR I.
HULK, YOU TEND TO PANIC CIVILIANS ANYWAY. CAN YOU JUMP SPIDER-MAN BACK TO NEW YORK WITHOUT DROPPING HIM?
--YOU CAN PRETEND YOU'RE MY ABUSIVE BOYFRIEND--?
YEEOW--!!

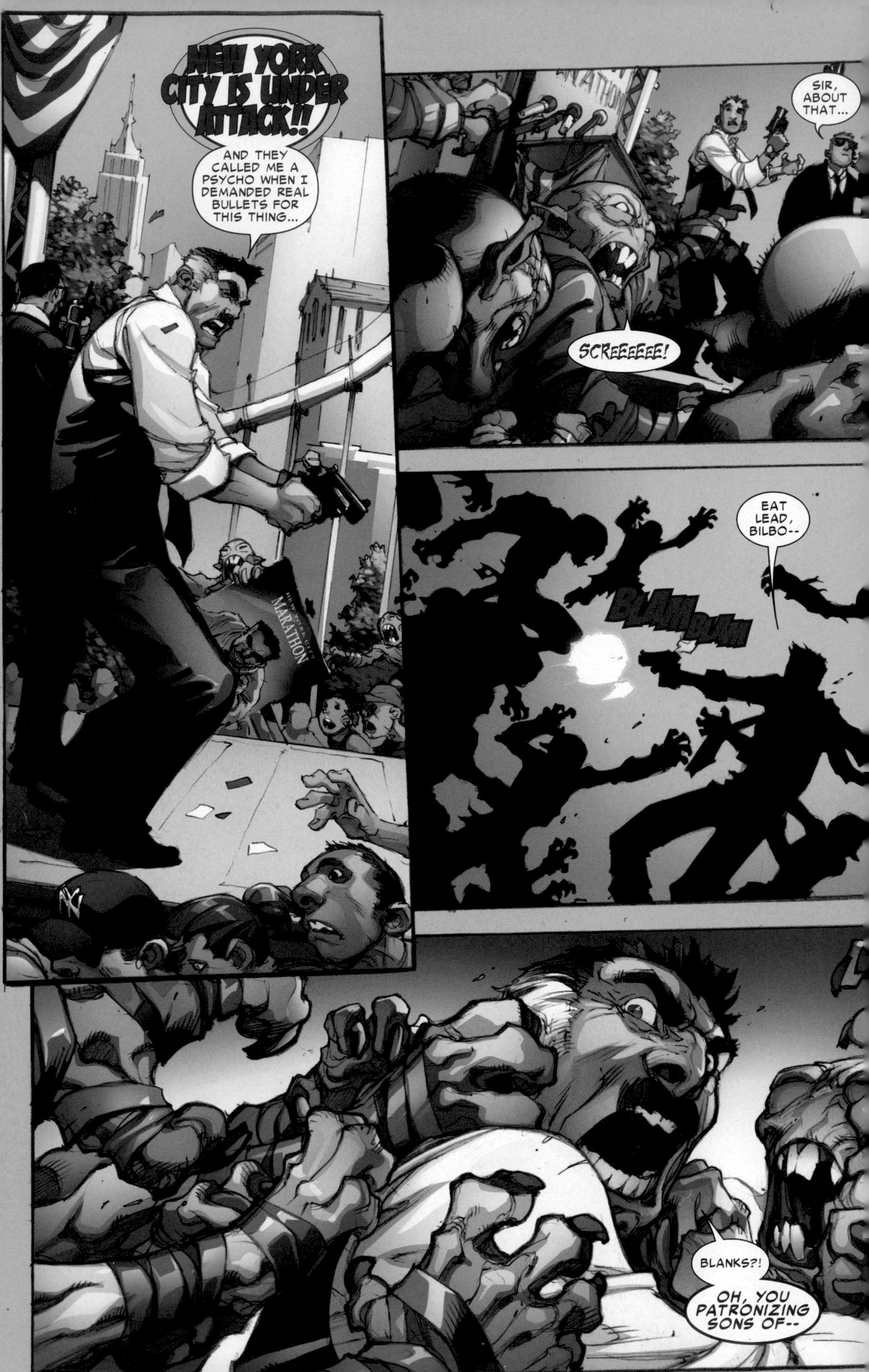
NEW YORK CITY IS UNDER ATTACK!!
AND THEY CALLED ME A PSYCHO WHEN I DEMANDED REAL BULLETS FOR THIS THING...
MARATHON
SIR, ABOUT THAT...
SCREEEEEE!
EAT LEAD, BILBO--
BLAM BLAM
BLANKS?!
OH, YOU PATRONIZING SONS OF--

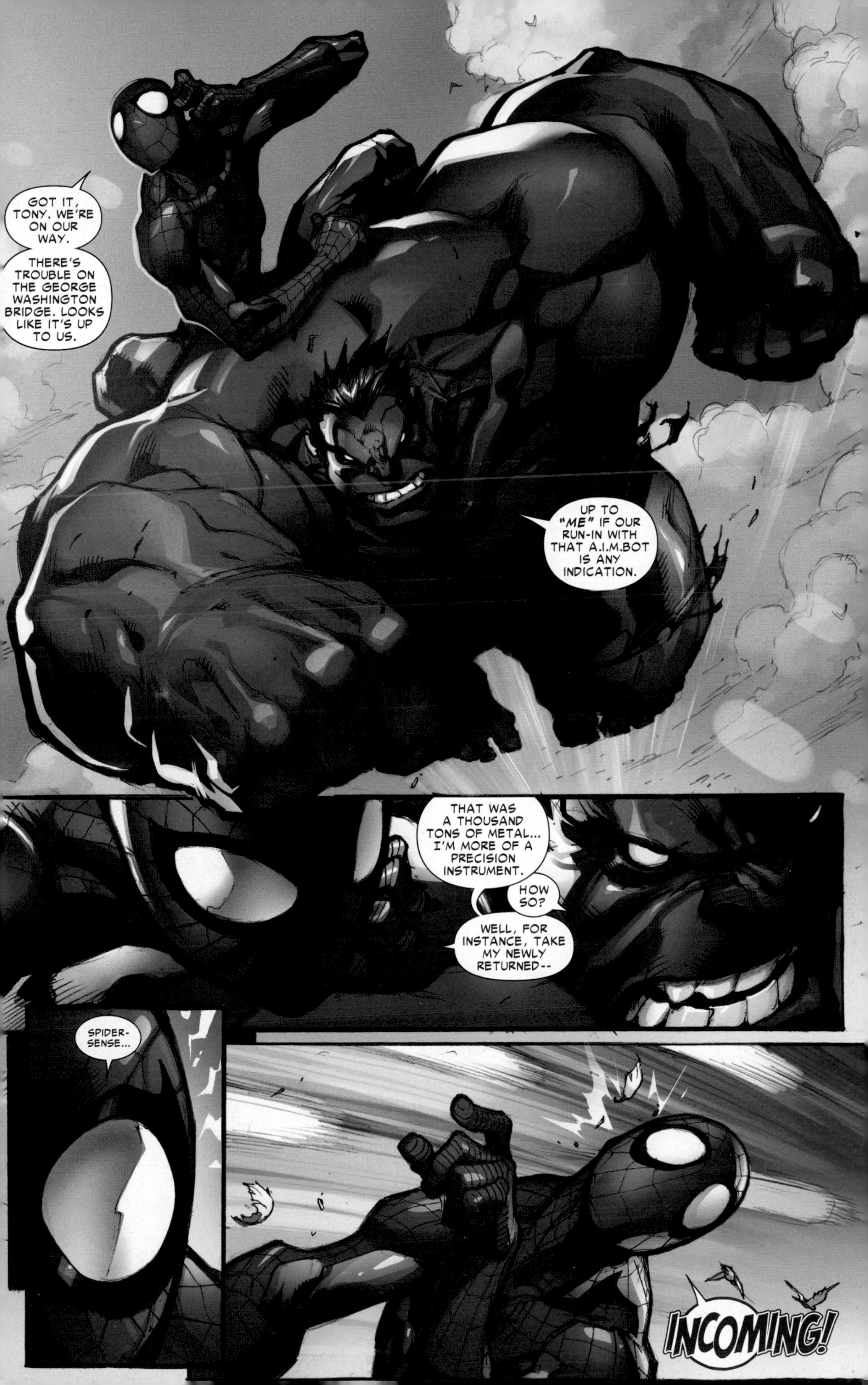
GOT IT, TONY. WE'RE ON OUR WAY.
THERE'S TROUBLE ON THE GEORGE WASHINGTON BRIDGE. LOOKS LIKE IT'S UP TO US.
UP TO "ME" IF OUR RUN-IN WITH THAT A.I.M.BOT IS ANY INDICATION.
THAT WAS A THOUSAND TONS OF METAL... I'M MORE OF A PRECISION INSTRUMENT.
HOW SO?
WELL, FOR INSTANCE, TAKE MY NEWLY RETURNED--
SPIDER-SENSE...
INCOMING!

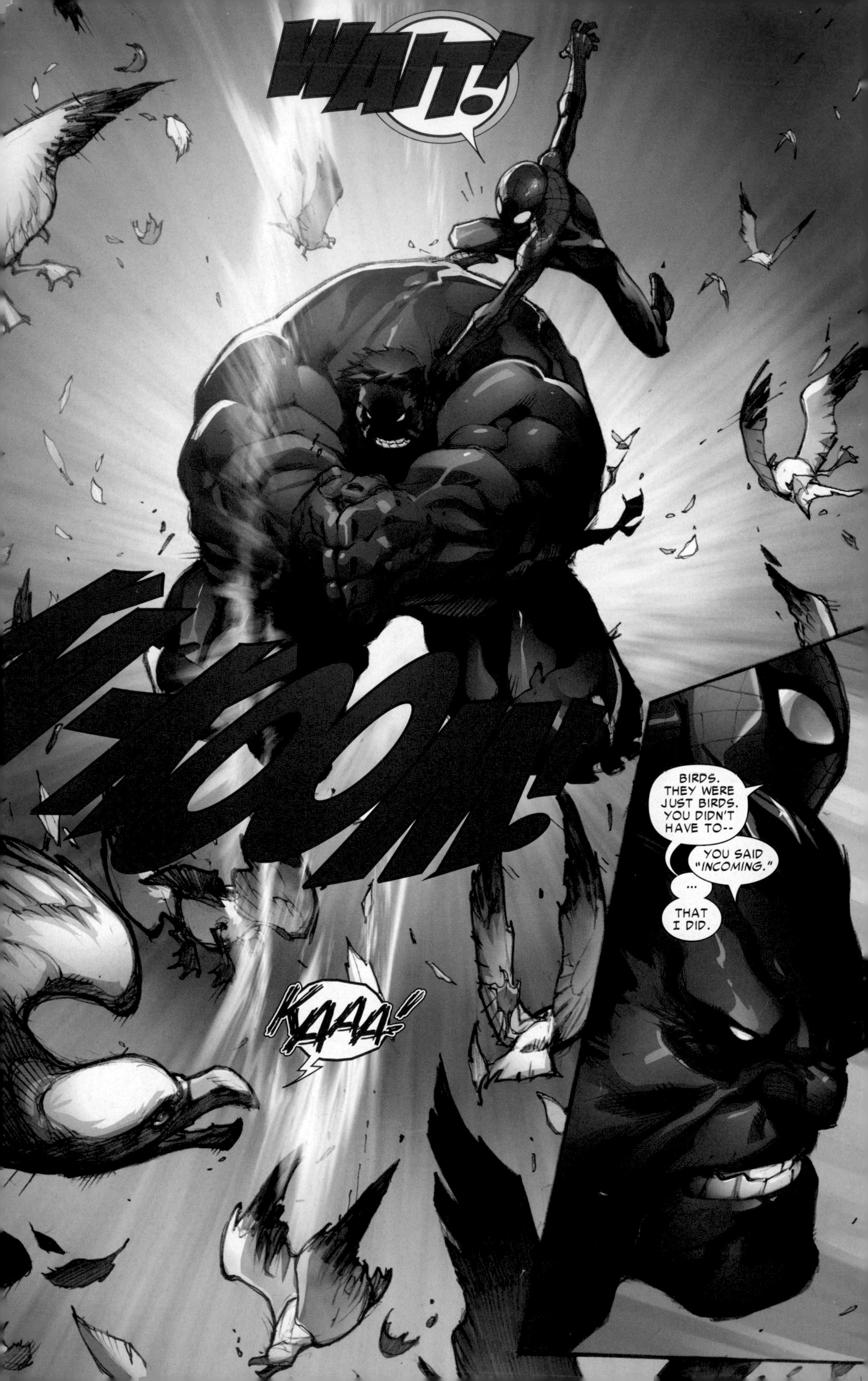
WAIT!
WHOOM!
KAAA!
BIRDS. THEY WERE JUST BIRDS. YOU DIDN'T HAVE TO--
YOU SAID "INCOMING."
...
THAT I DID.

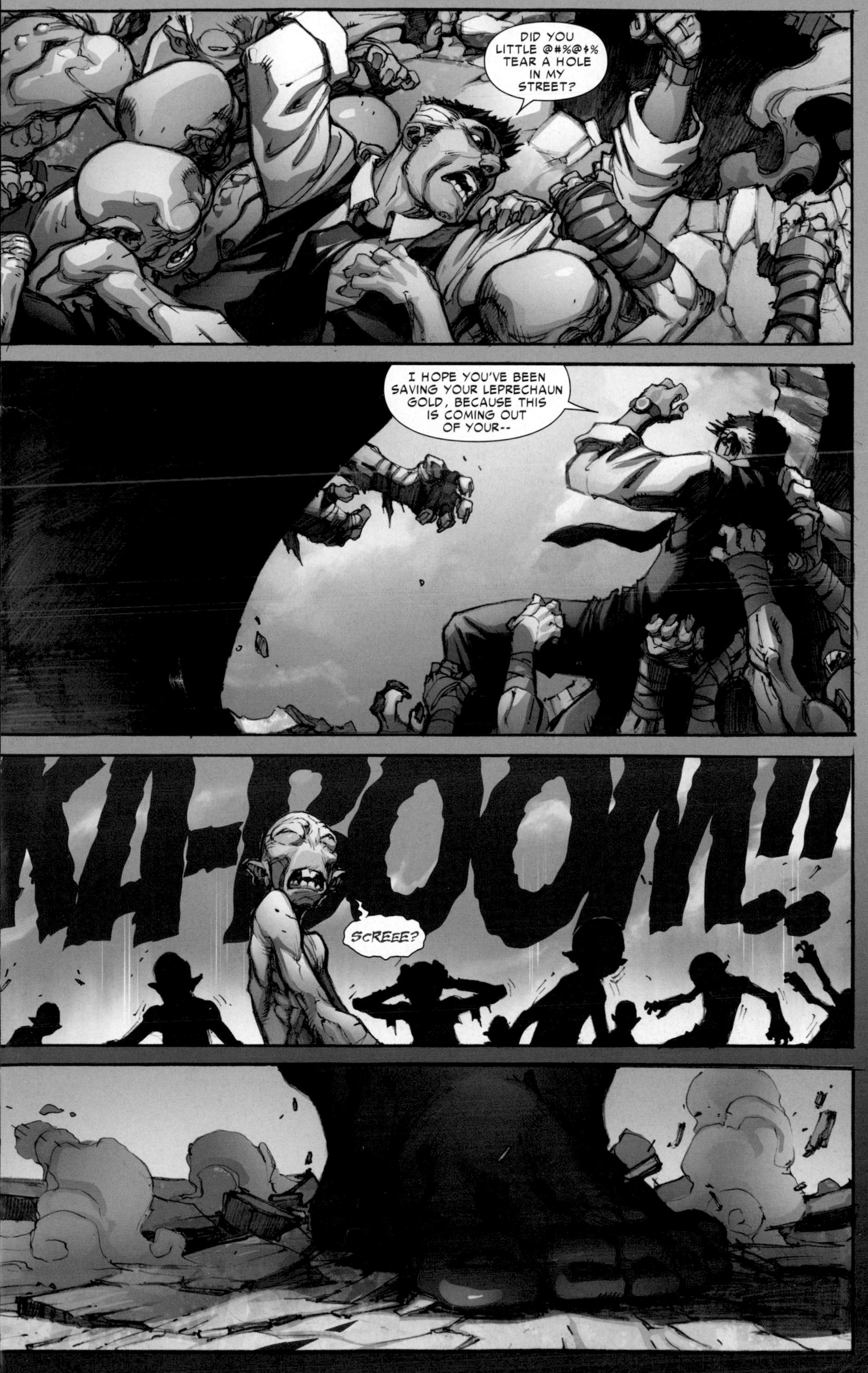
DID YOU LITTLE @#%@$% TEAR A HOLE IN MY STREET?
I HOPE YOU'VE BEEN SAVING YOUR LEPRECHAUN GOLD, BECAUSE THIS IS COMING OUT OF YOUR--
SCREEE?

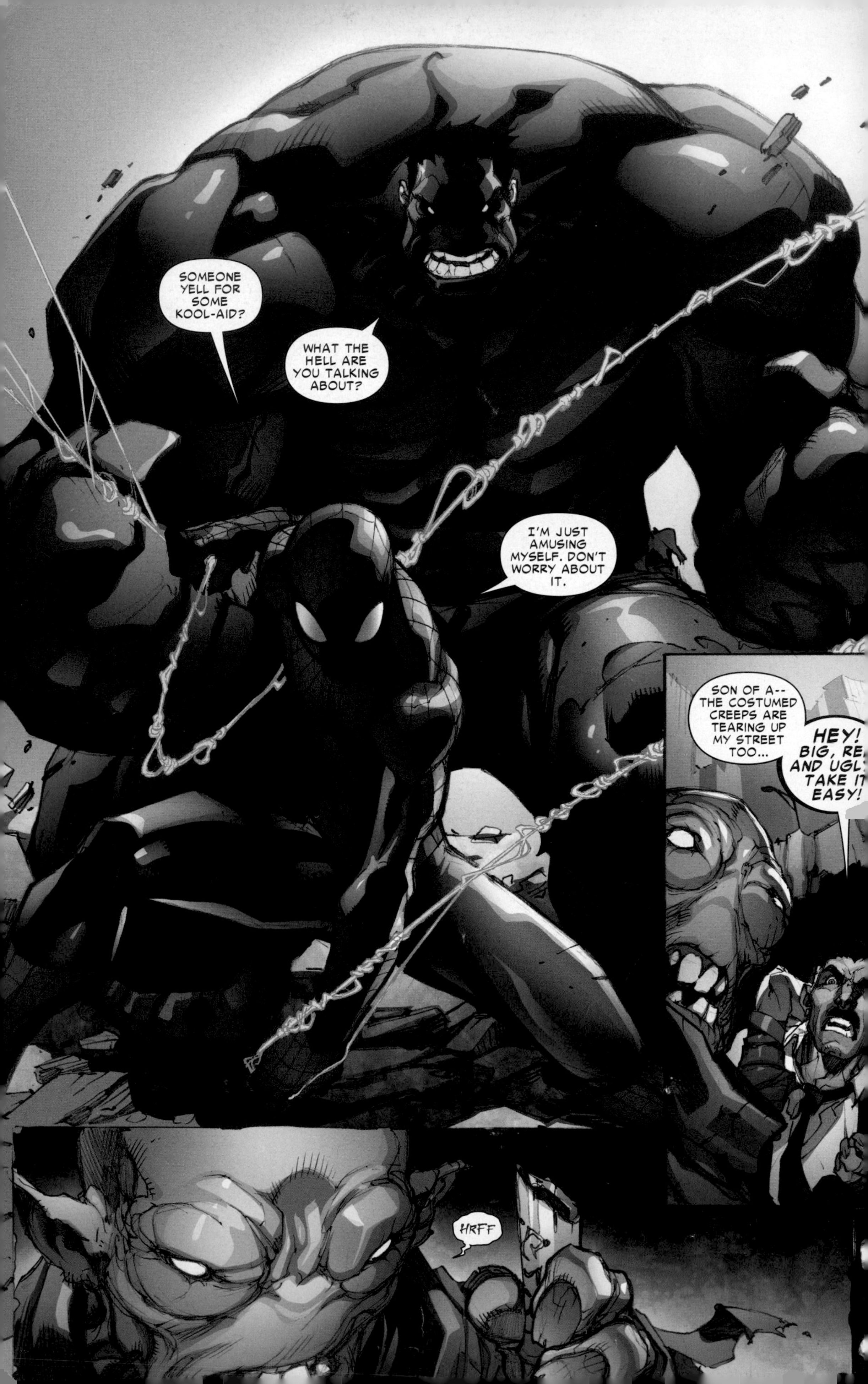
SOMEONE YELL FOR SOME KOOL-AID?
WHAT THE HELL ARE YOU TALKING ABOUT?
I'M JUST AMUSING MYSELF. DON'T WORRY ABOUT IT.
SON OF A-- THE COSTUMED CREEPS ARE TEARING UP MY STREET TOO...
HEY! BIG, RE AND UGL TAKE IT EASY!
HRFF

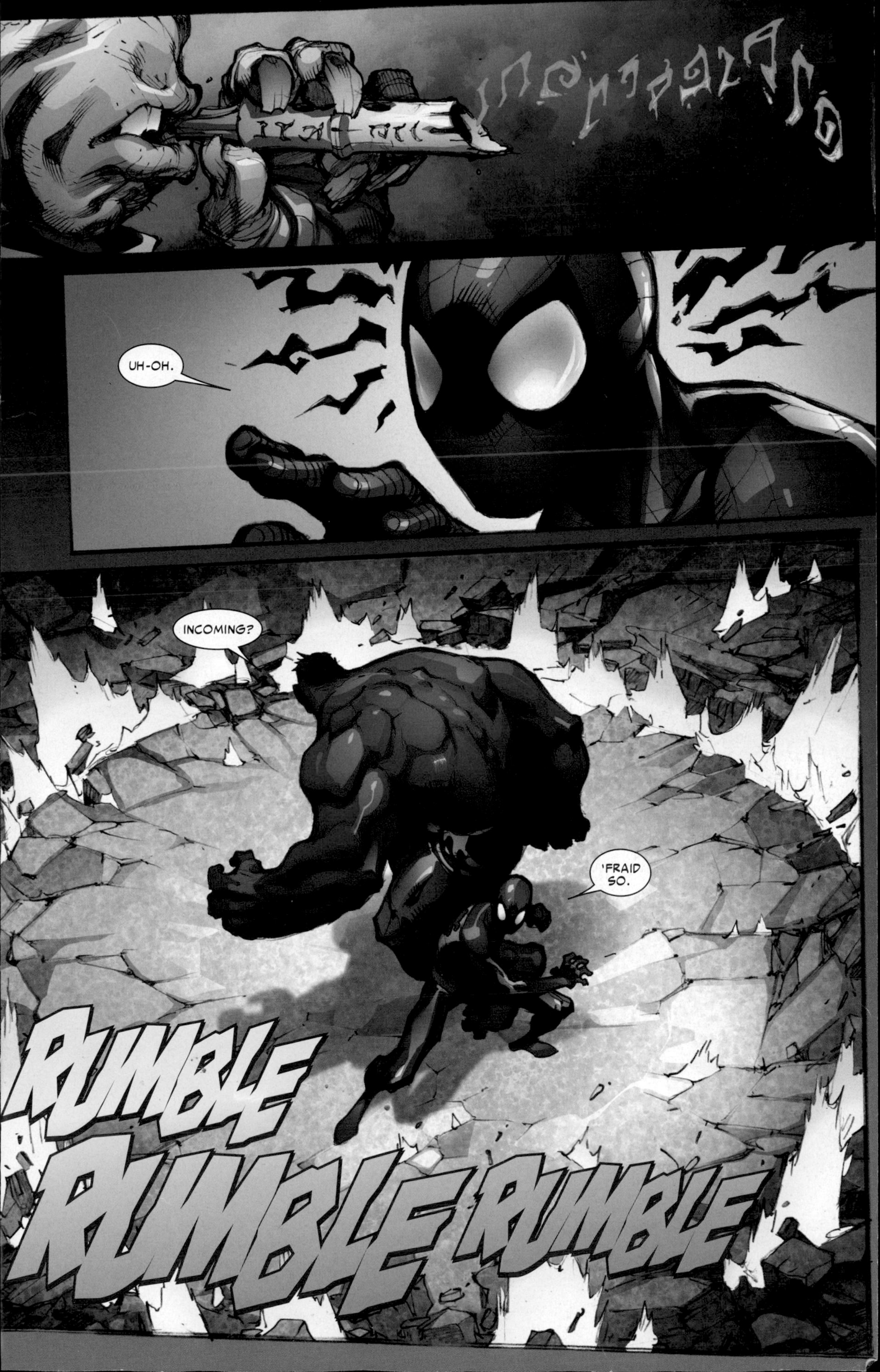
UH-OH.
INCOMING?
'FRAID SO.
RUMBLE
RUMBLE RUMBLE

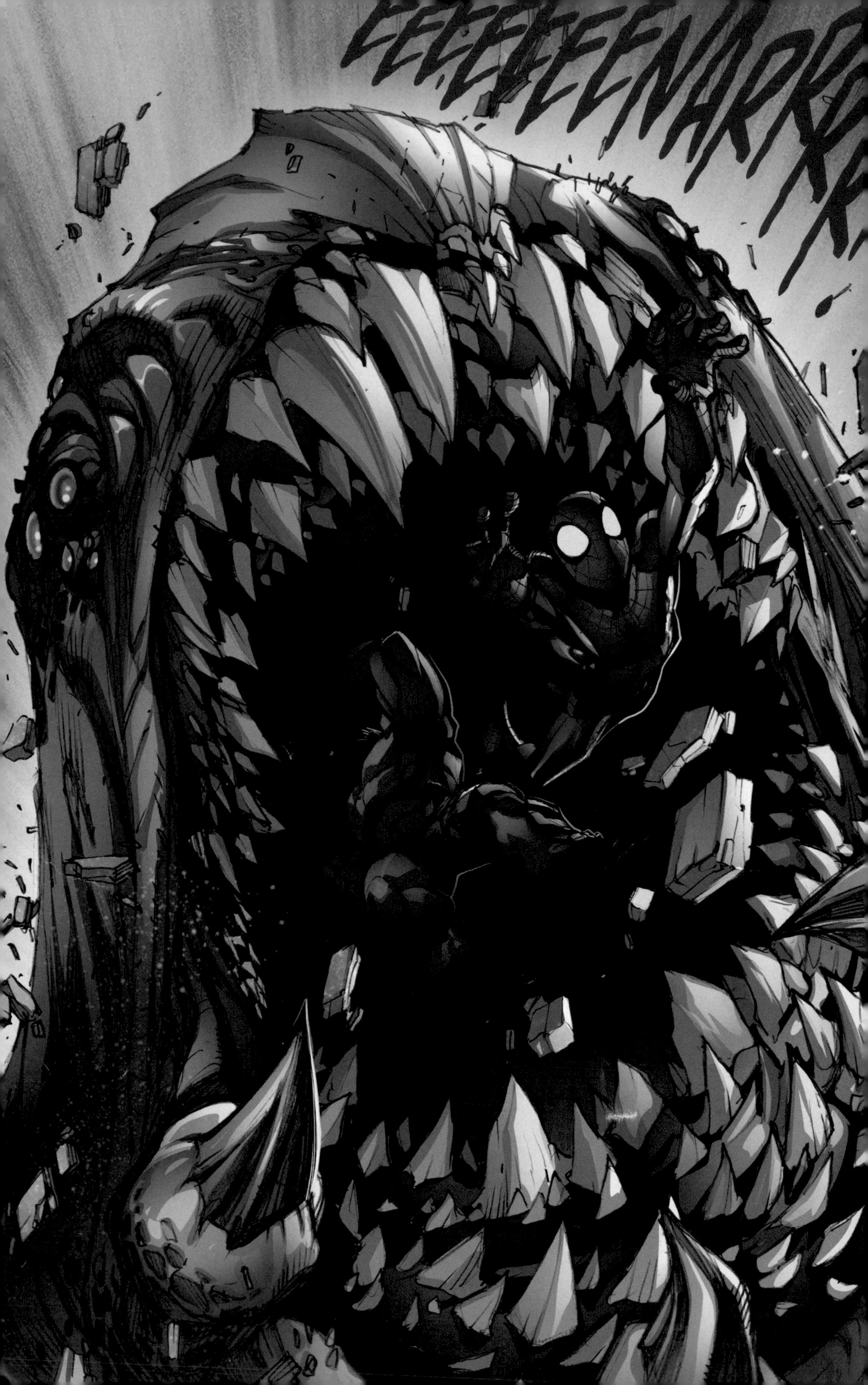

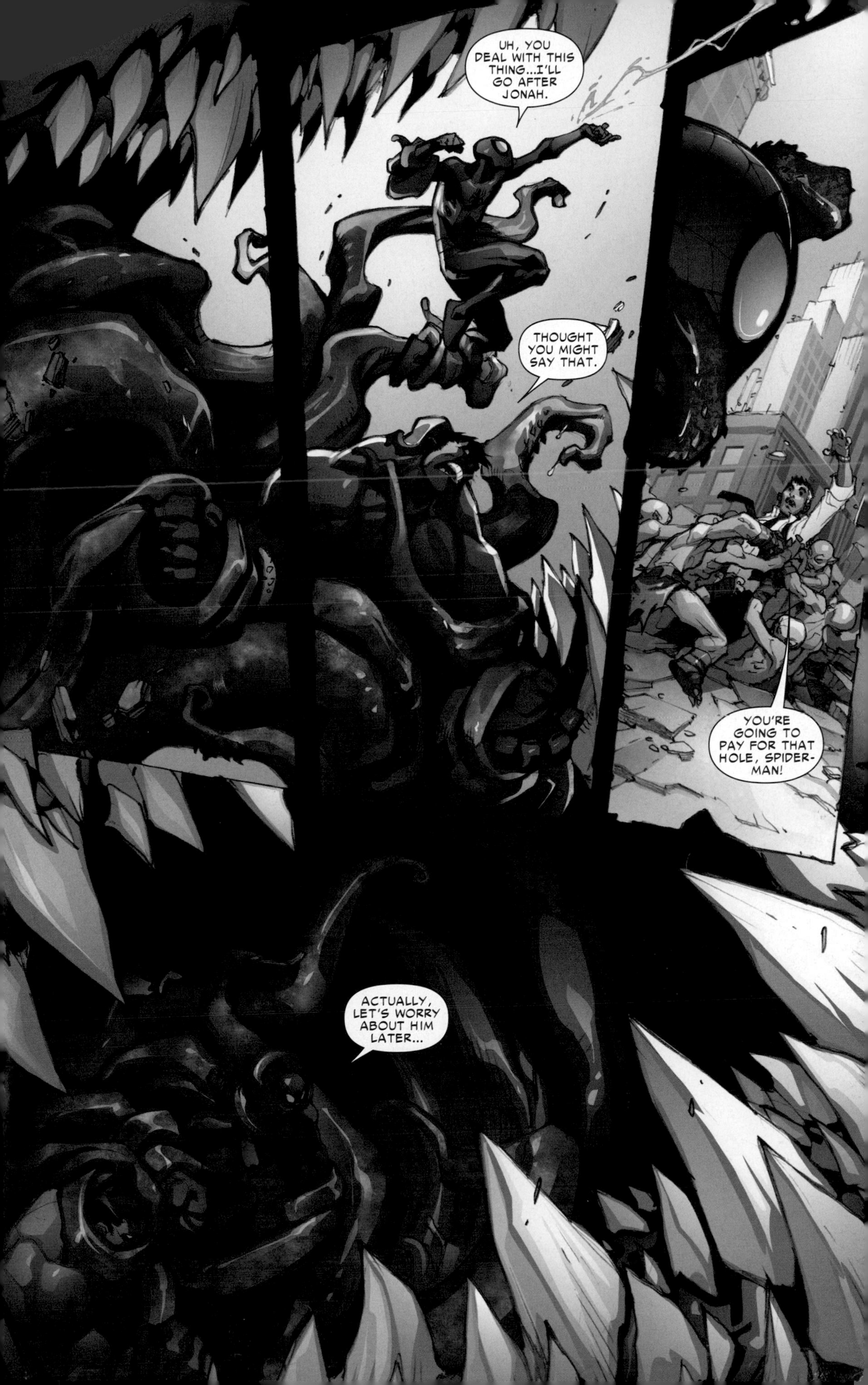
UH, YOU DEAL WITH THIS THING...I'LL GO AFTER JONAH.
THOUGHT YOU MIGHT SAY THAT.
YOU'RE GOING TO PAY FOR THAT HOLE, SPIDER-MAN!
ACTUALLY, LET'S WORRY ABOUT HIM LATER...

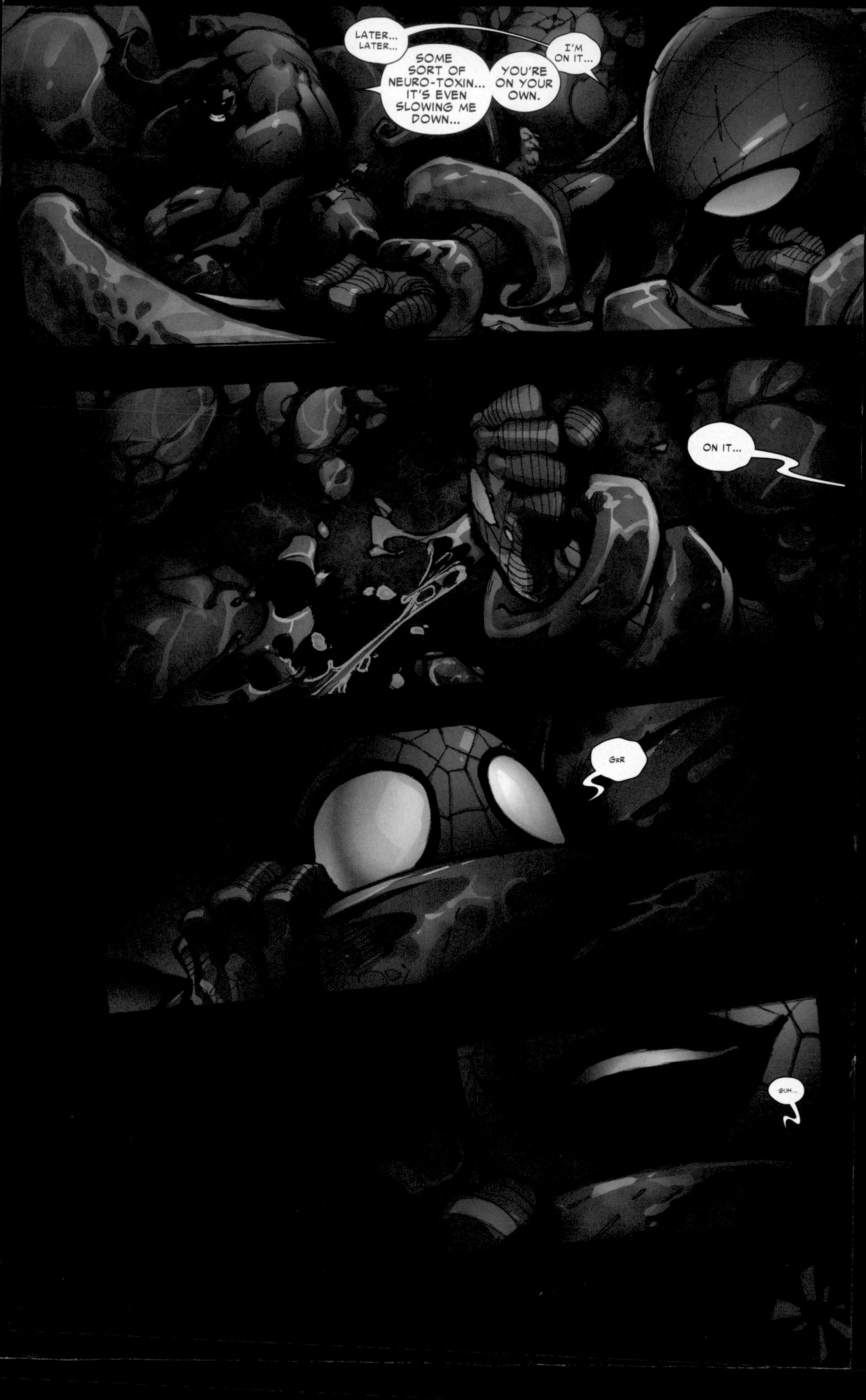
LATER... LATER...
SOME SORT OF NEURO-TOXIN... IT'S EVEN SLOWING ME DOWN...
YOU'RE ON YOUR OWN.
I'M ON IT...
ON IT...
GRR
GUH...

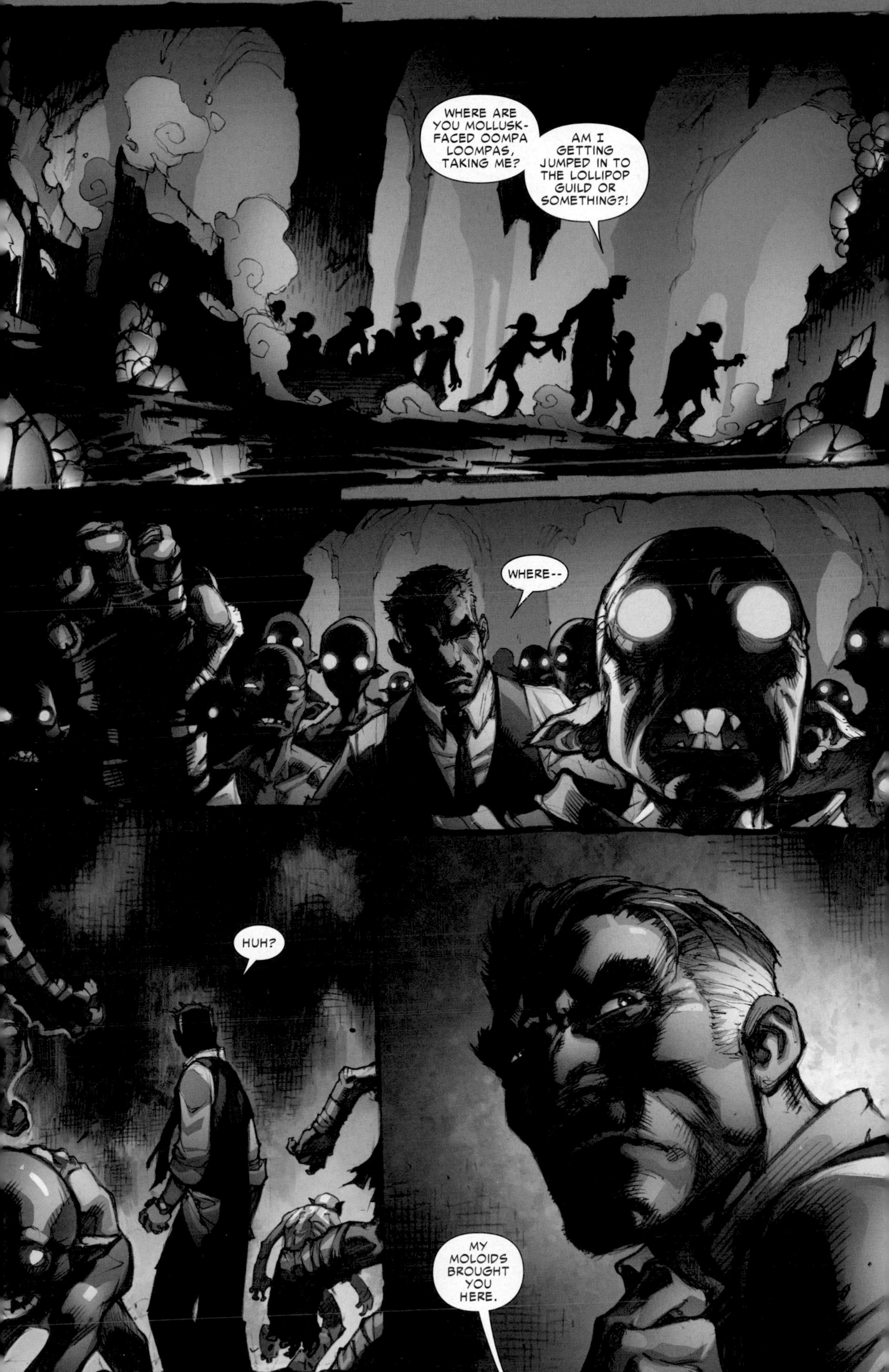
WHERE ARE YOU MOLLUSK-FACED OOMPA LOOMPAS, TAKING ME?
AM I GETTING JUMPED IN TO THE LOLLIPOP GUILD OR SOMETHING?!
WHERE--
HUH?
MY MOLOIDS BROUGHT YOU HERE.

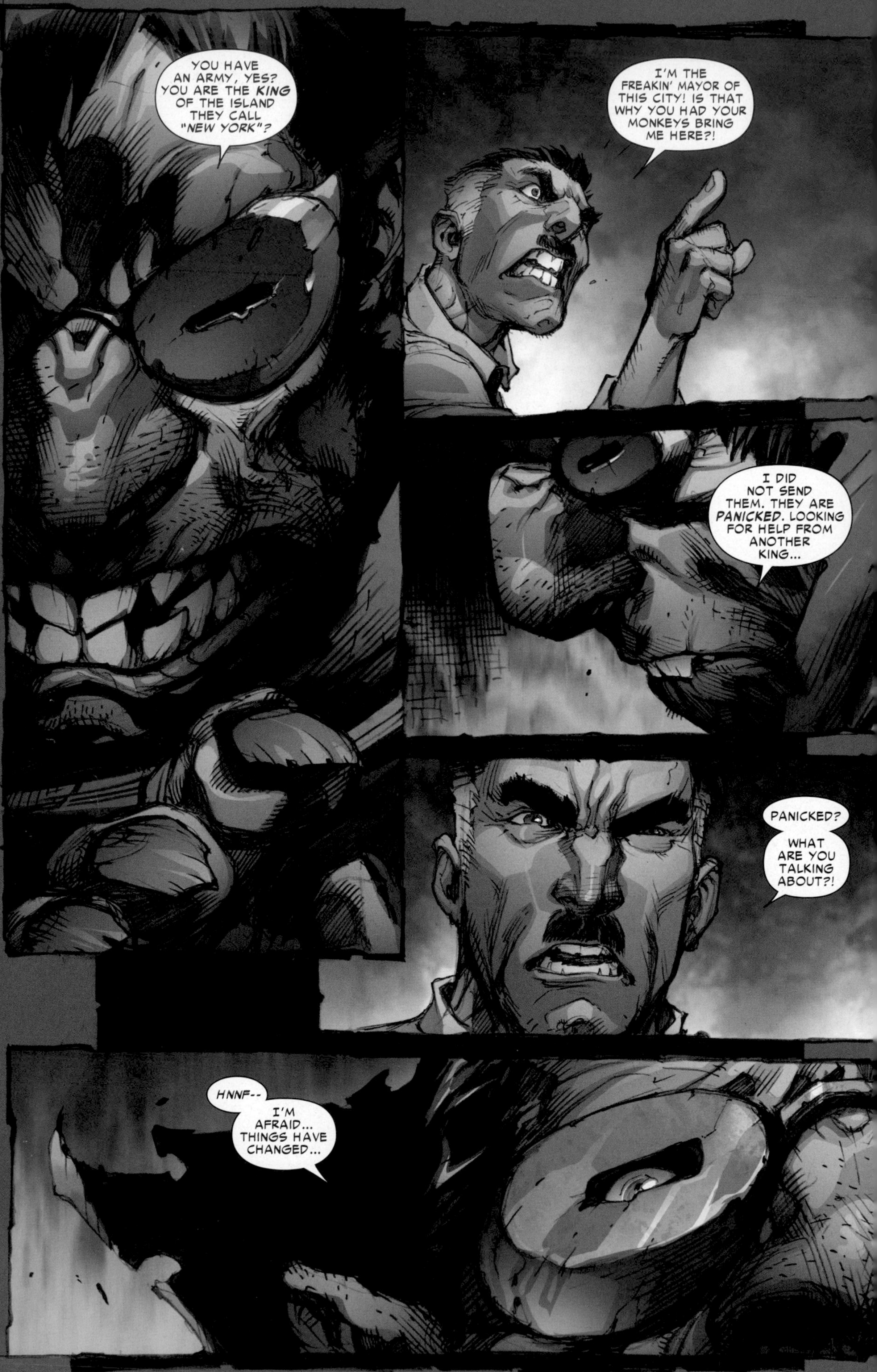
YOU HAVE AN ARMY, YES? YOU ARE THE *KING* OF THE ISLAND THEY CALL *"NEW YORK"*?
I'M THE FREAKIN' MAYOR OF THIS CITY! IS THAT WHY YOU HAD YOUR MONKEYS BRING ME HERE?!
I DID NOT SEND THEM. THEY ARE *PANICKED*. LOOKING FOR HELP FROM ANOTHER KING...
PANICKED?
WHAT ARE YOU TALKING ABOUT?!
HNNF--
I'M AFRAID... THINGS HAVE CHANGED...

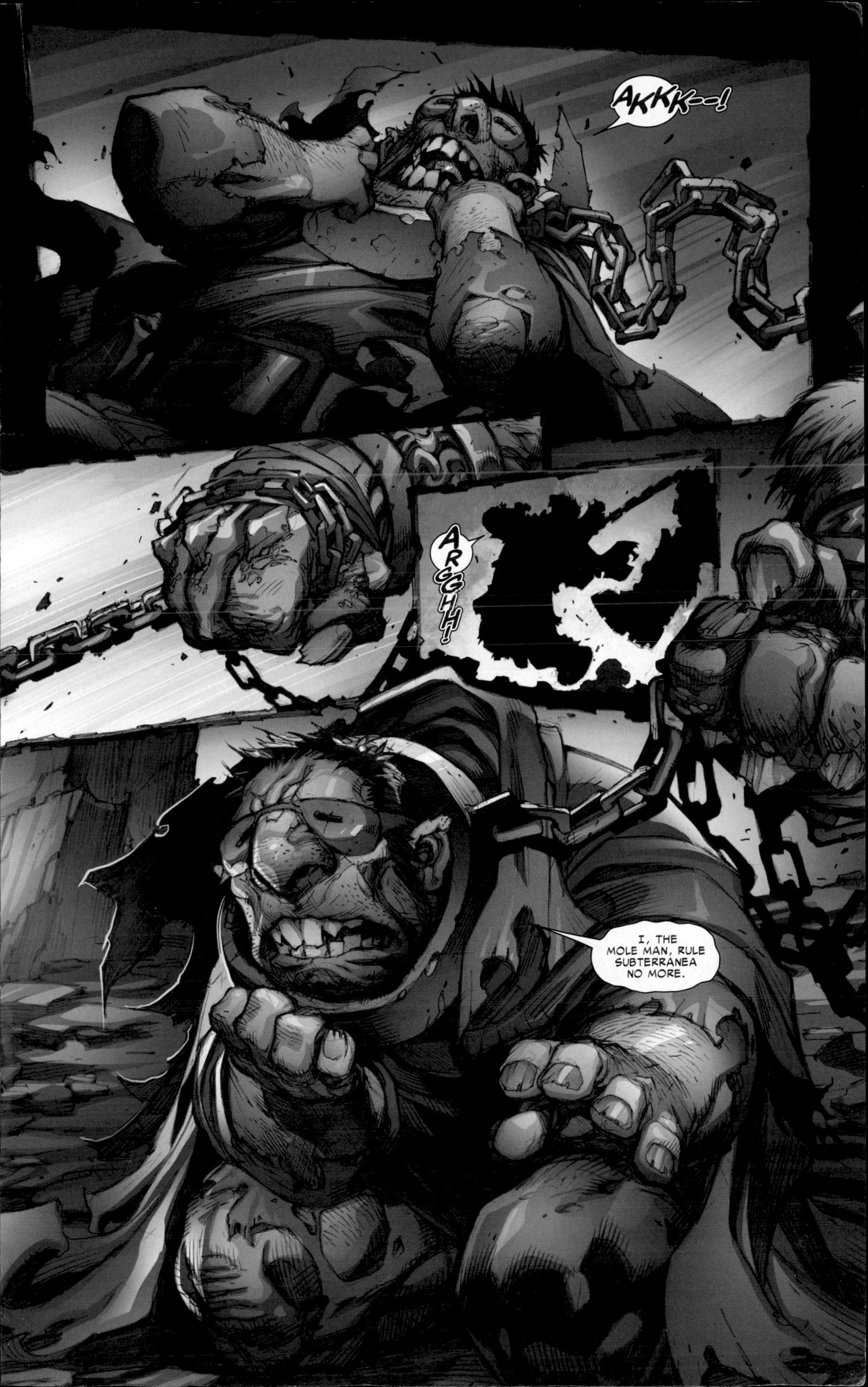
AKKK--!
ARGGHH!
I, THE MOLE MAN, RULE SUBTERRANEA NO MORE.

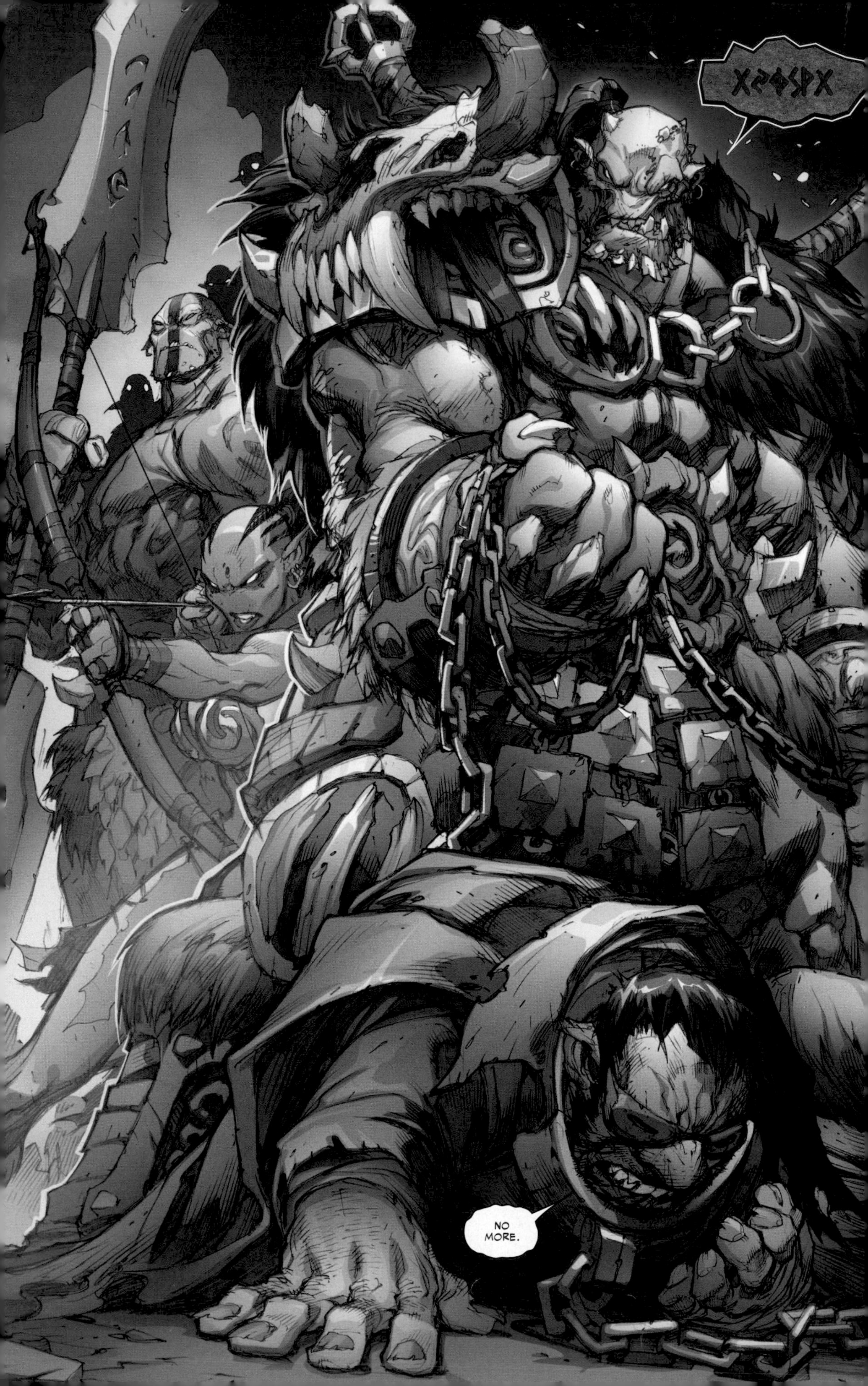
NO MORE.

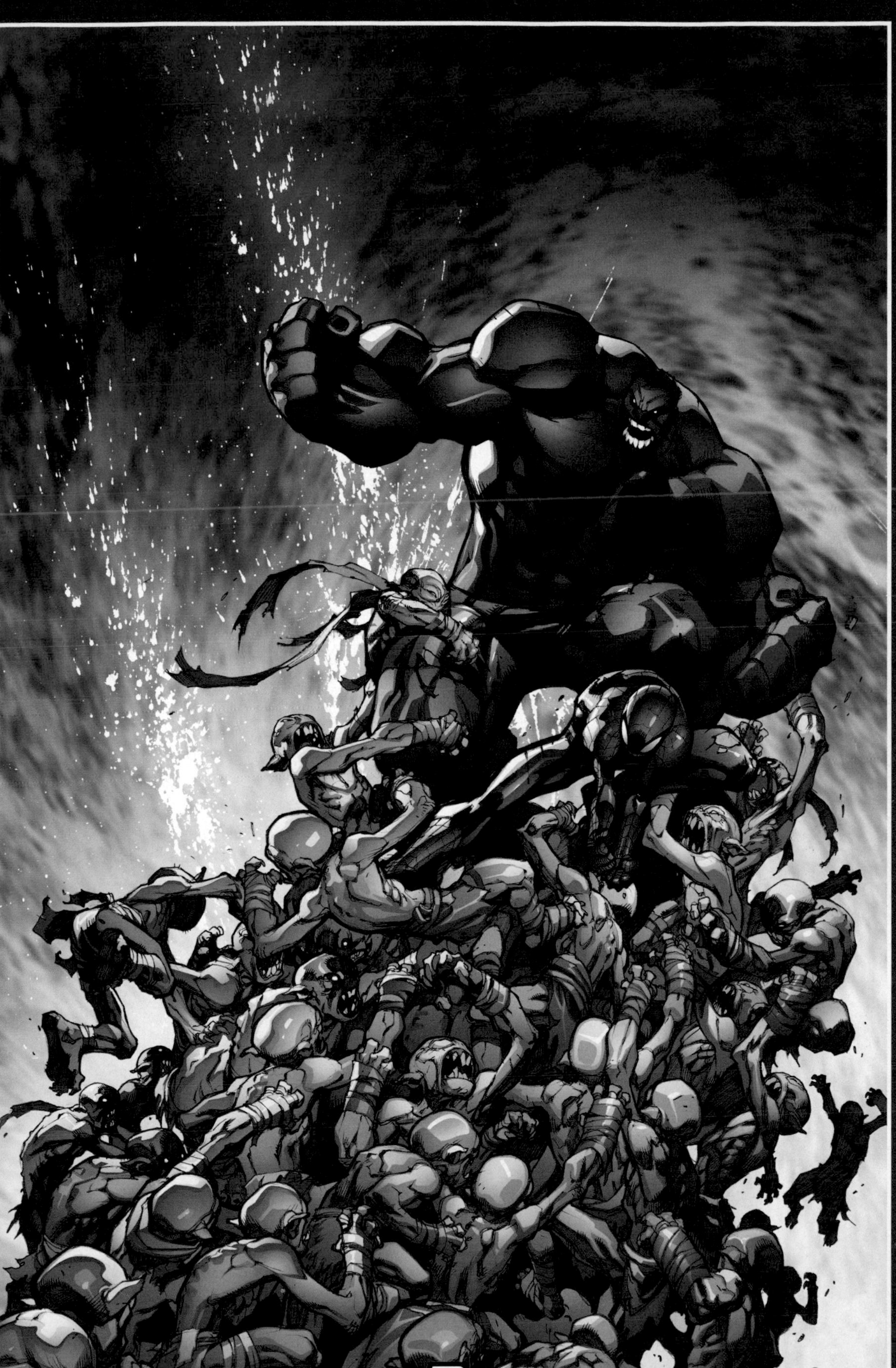

2

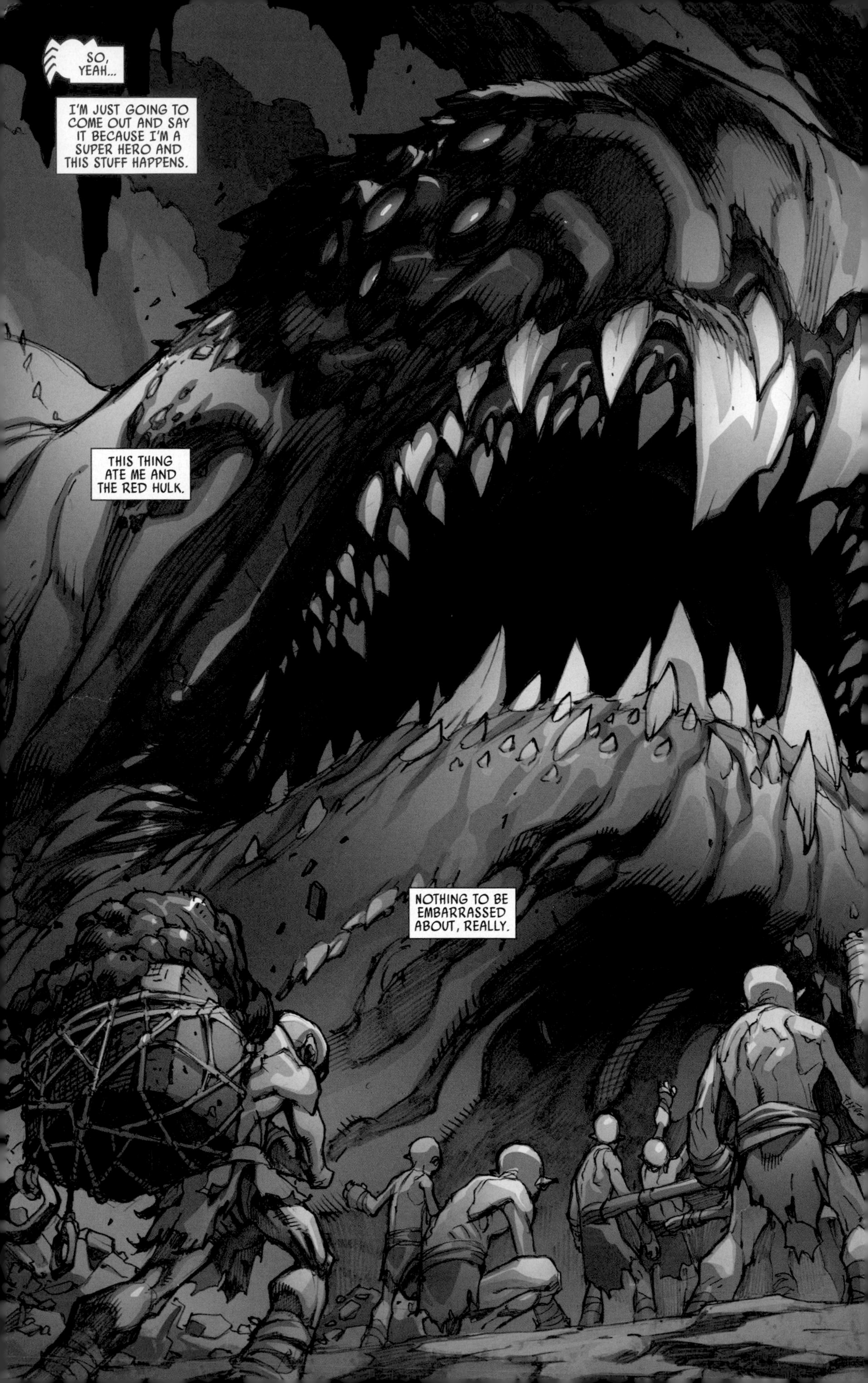
SO, YEAH...
I'M JUST GOING TO COME OUT AND SAY IT BECAUSE I'M A SUPER HERO AND THIS STUFF HAPPENS.
THIS THING ATE ME AND THE RED HULK.
NOTHING TO BE EMBARRASSED ABOUT, REALLY.

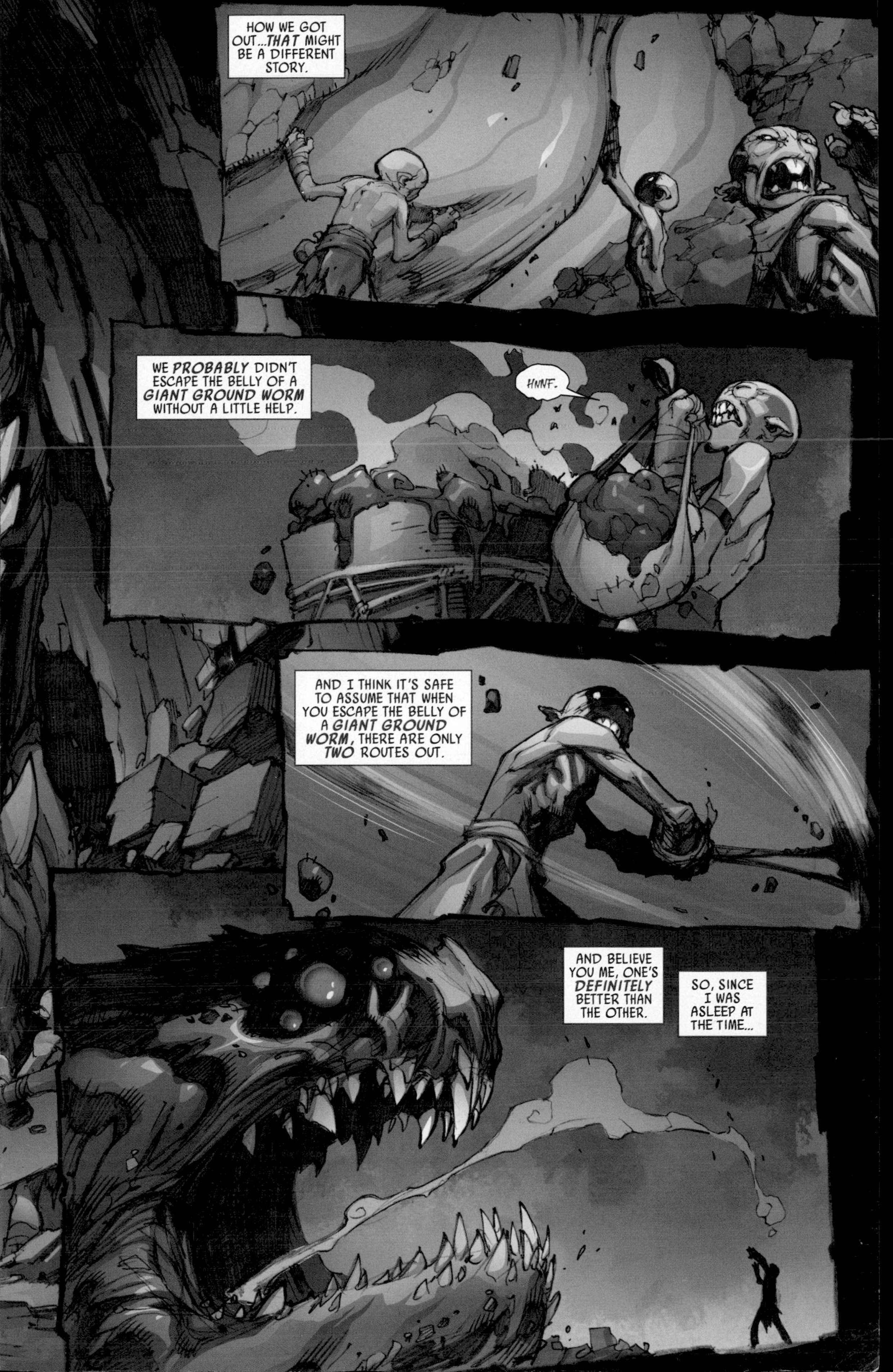
HOW WE GOT OUT...THAT MIGHT BE A DIFFERENT STORY.
WE PROBABLY DIDN'T ESCAPE THE BELLY OF A GIANT GROUND WORM WITHOUT A LITTLE HELP.
HNNF.
AND I THINK IT'S SAFE TO ASSUME THAT WHEN YOU ESCAPE THE BELLY OF A GIANT GROUND WORM, THERE ARE ONLY TWO ROUTES OUT.
AND BELIEVE YOU ME, ONE'S DEFINITELY BETTER THAN THE OTHER.
SO, SINCE I WAS ASLEEP AT THE TIME...

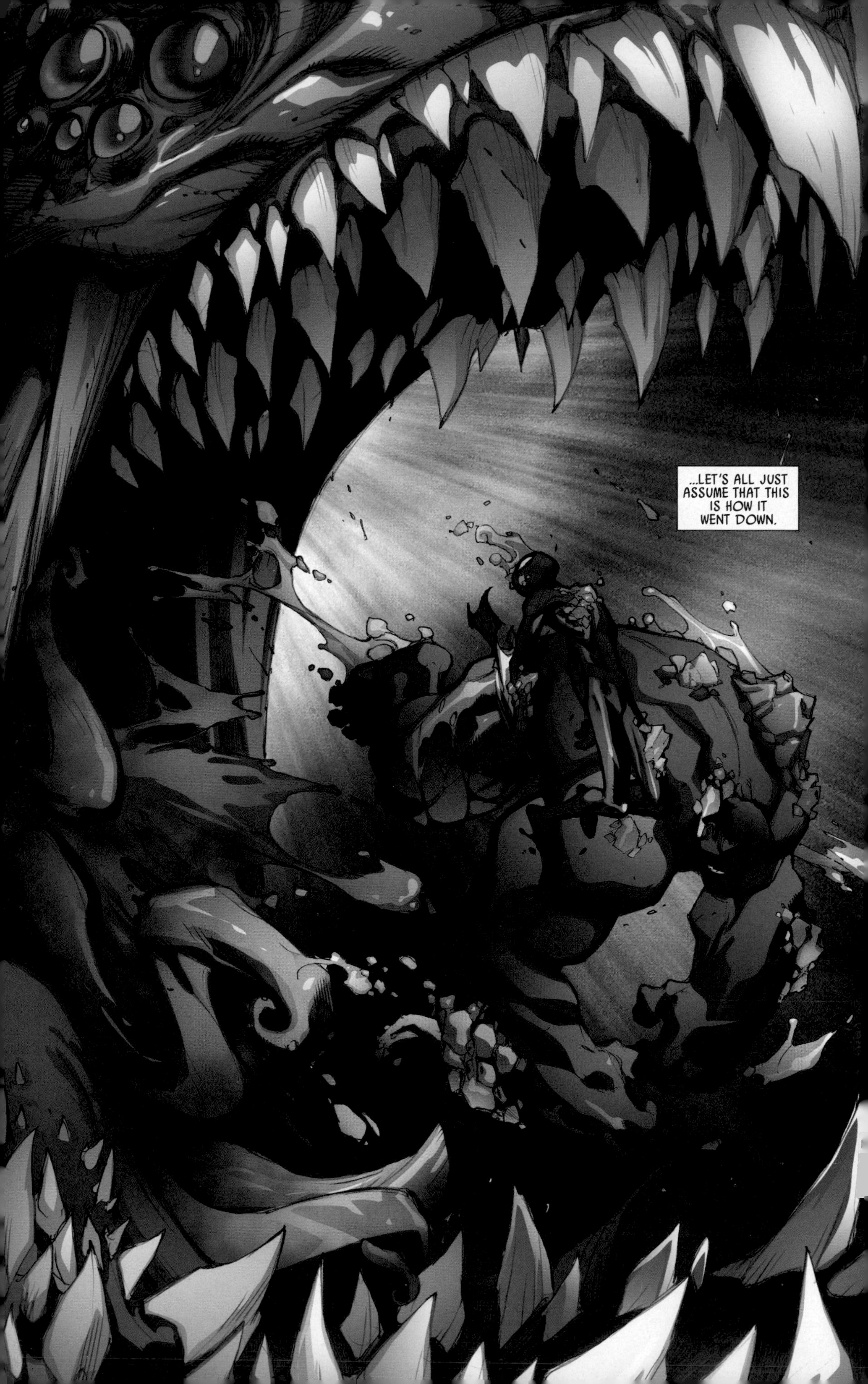
...LET'S ALL JUST ASSUME THAT THIS IS HOW IT WENT DOWN.

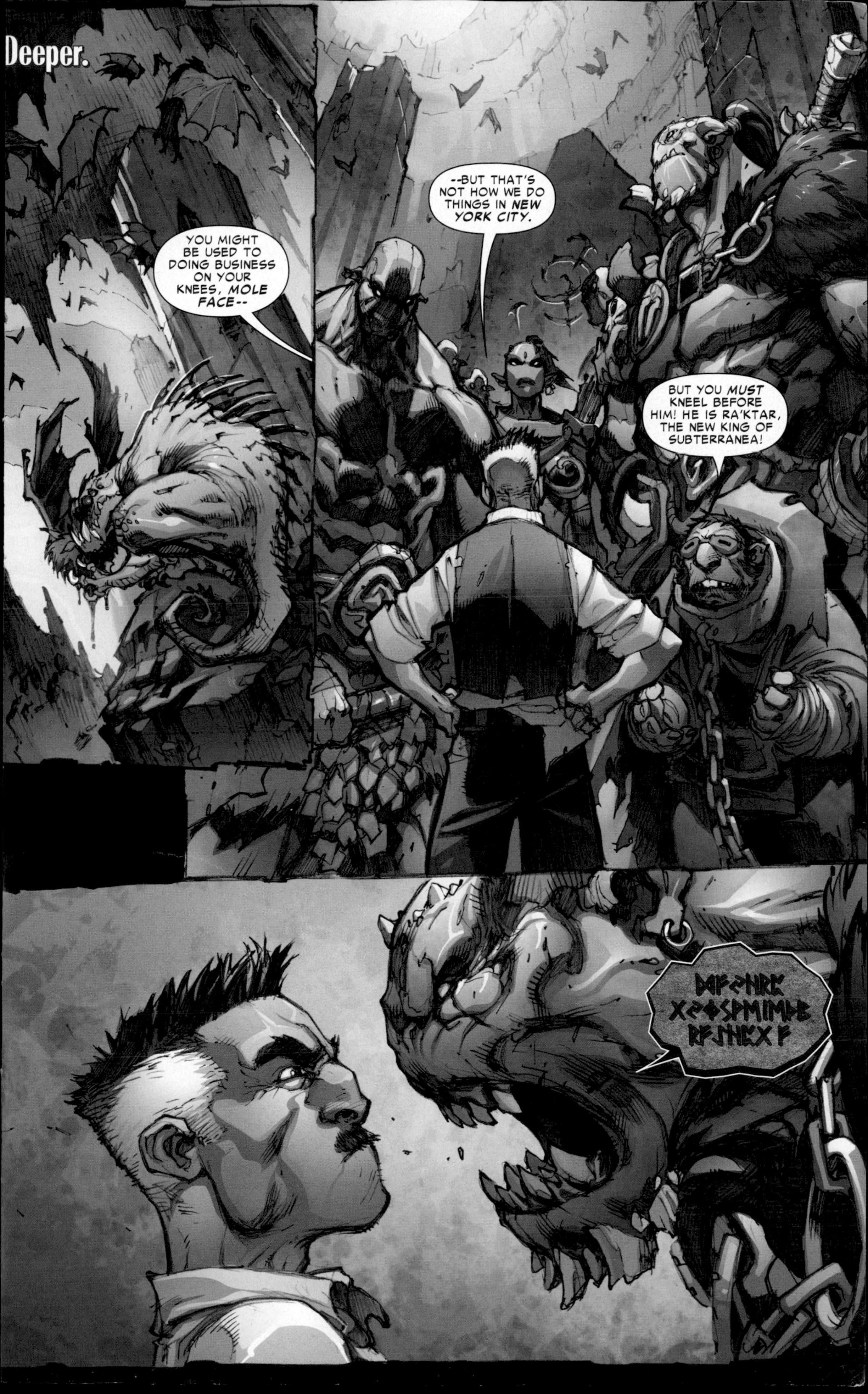
Deeper.
YOU MIGHT BE USED TO DOING BUSINESS ON YOUR KNEES, MOLE FACE--
--BUT THAT'S NOT HOW WE DO THINGS IN NEW YORK CITY.
BUT YOU MUST KNEEL BEFORE HIM! HE IS RA'KTAR, THE NEW KING OF SUBTERRANEA!

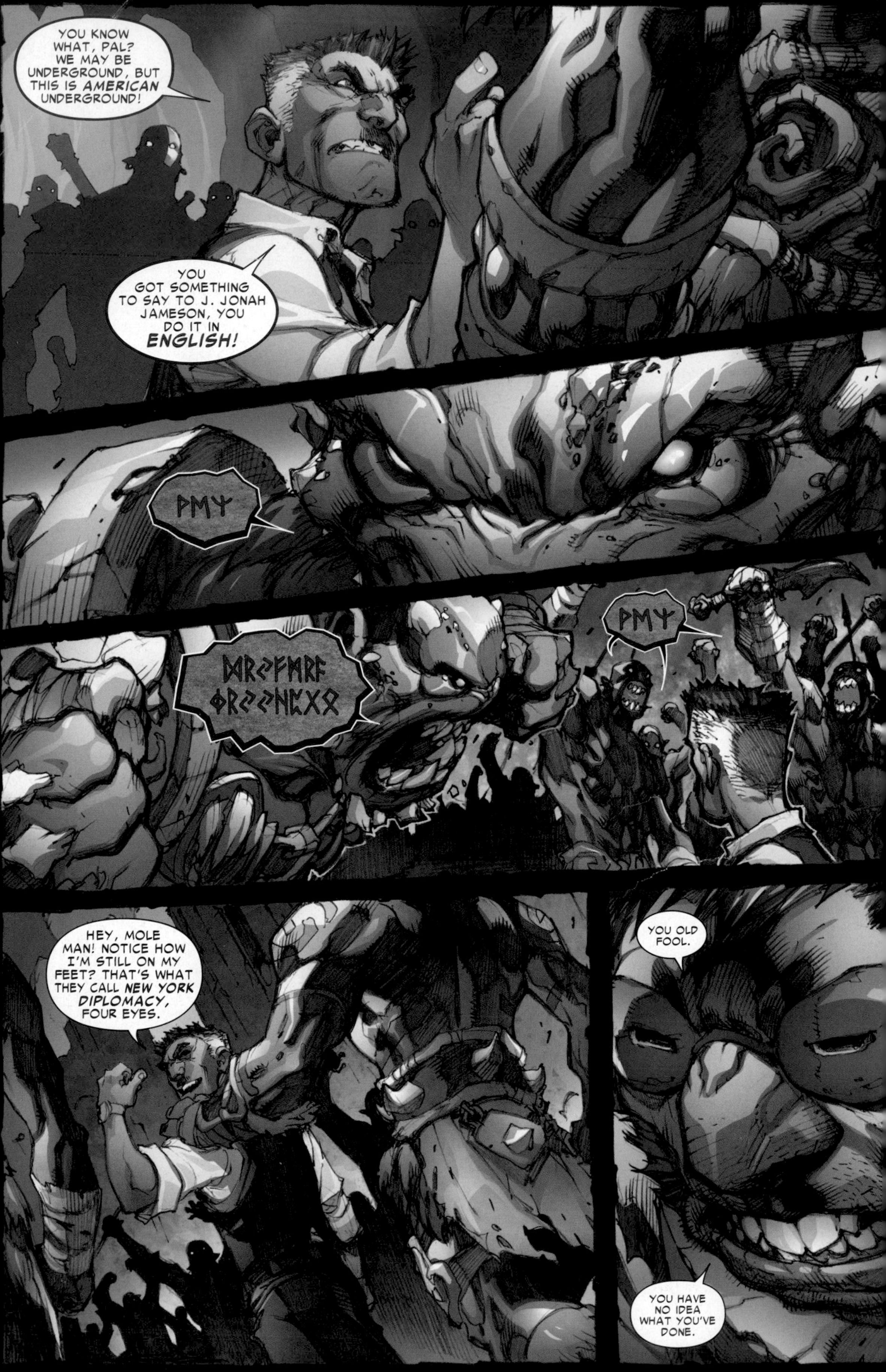
YOU KNOW WHAT, PAL? WE MAY BE UNDERGROUND, BUT THIS IS *AMERICAN* UNDERGROUND!
YOU GOT SOMETHING TO SAY TO J. JONAH JAMESON, YOU DO IT IN **ENGLISH!**
HEY, MOLE MAN! NOTICE HOW I'M STILL ON MY FEET? THAT'S WHAT THEY CALL *NEW YORK DIPLOMACY*, FOUR EYES.
YOU OLD FOOL.
YOU HAVE NO IDEA WHAT YOU'VE DONE.

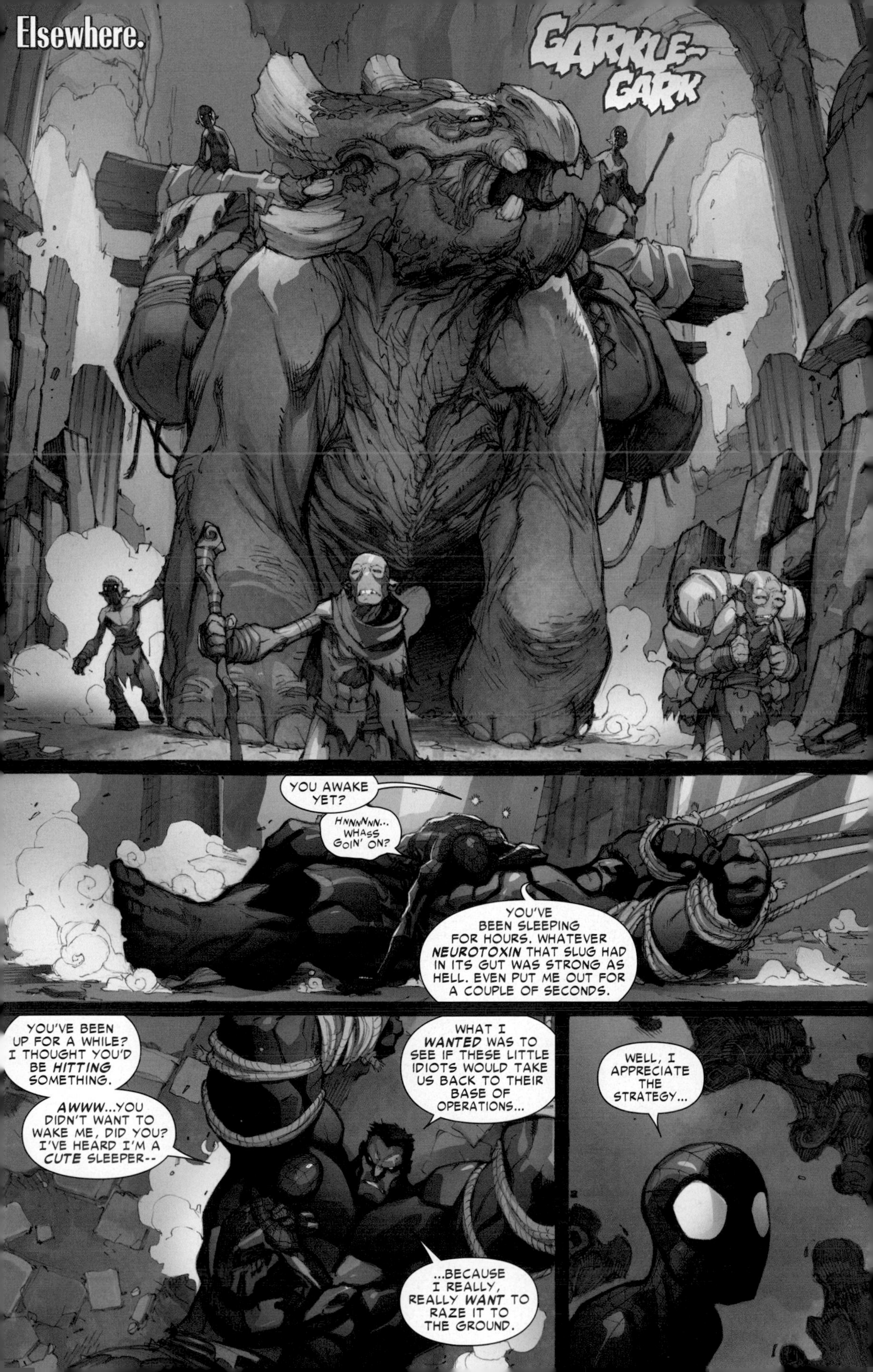
Elsewhere.
GARKLE-GARK
YOU AWAKE YET?
HNNNNNN... WHASS GOIN' ON?
YOU'VE BEEN SLEEPING FOR HOURS. WHATEVER NEUROTOXIN THAT SLUG HAD IN ITS GUT WAS STRONG AS HELL. EVEN PUT ME OUT FOR A COUPLE OF SECONDS.
YOU'VE BEEN UP FOR A WHILE? I THOUGHT YOU'D BE HITTING SOMETHING.
AWWW...YOU DIDN'T WANT TO WAKE ME, DID YOU? I'VE HEARD I'M A CUTE SLEEPER--
WHAT I WANTED WAS TO SEE IF THESE LITTLE IDIOTS WOULD TAKE US BACK TO THEIR BASE OF OPERATIONS...
...BECAUSE I REALLY, REALLY WANT TO RAZE IT TO THE GROUND.
WELL, I APPRECIATE THE STRATEGY...

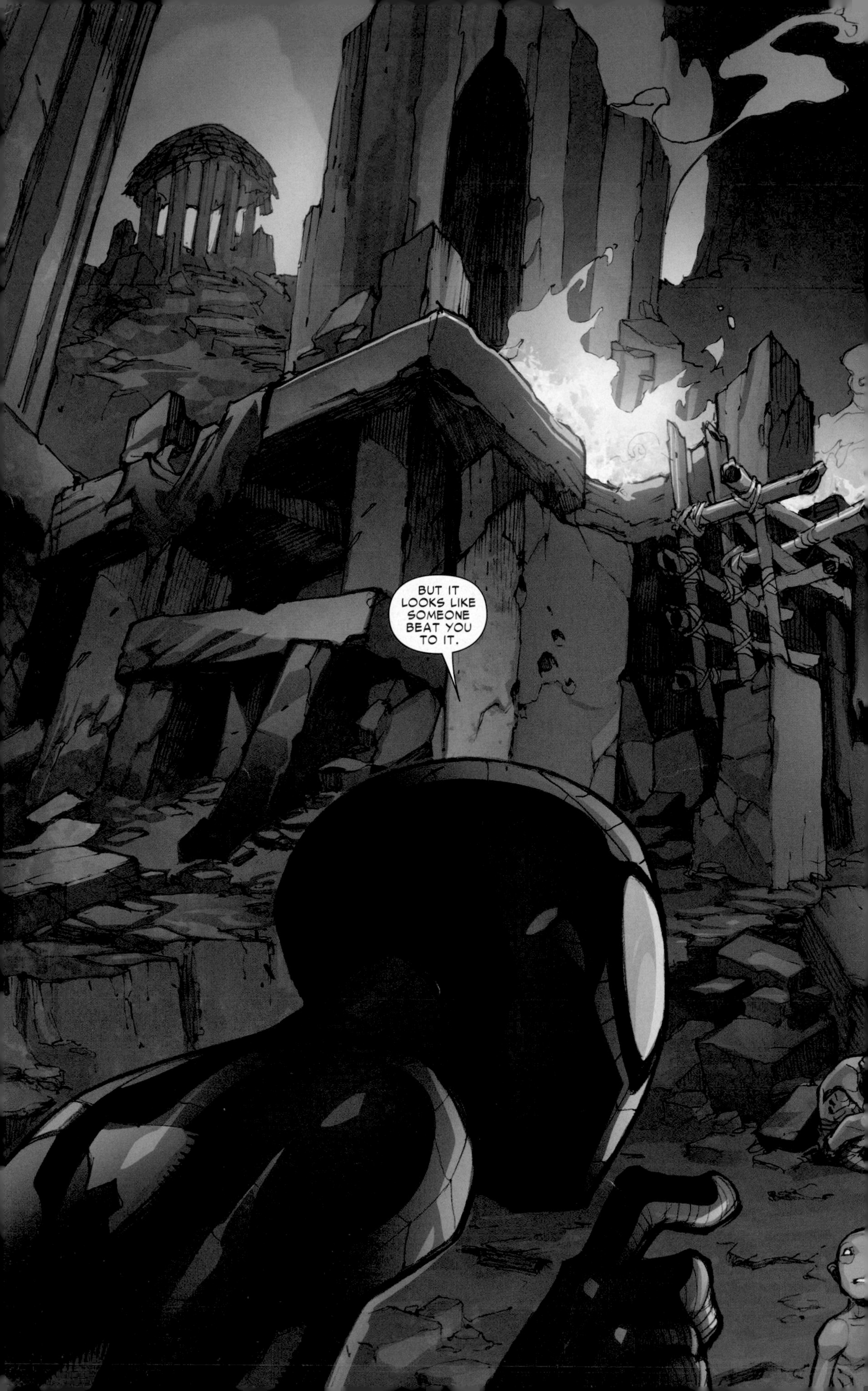
BUT IT LOOKS LIKE SOMEONE BEAT YOU TO IT.

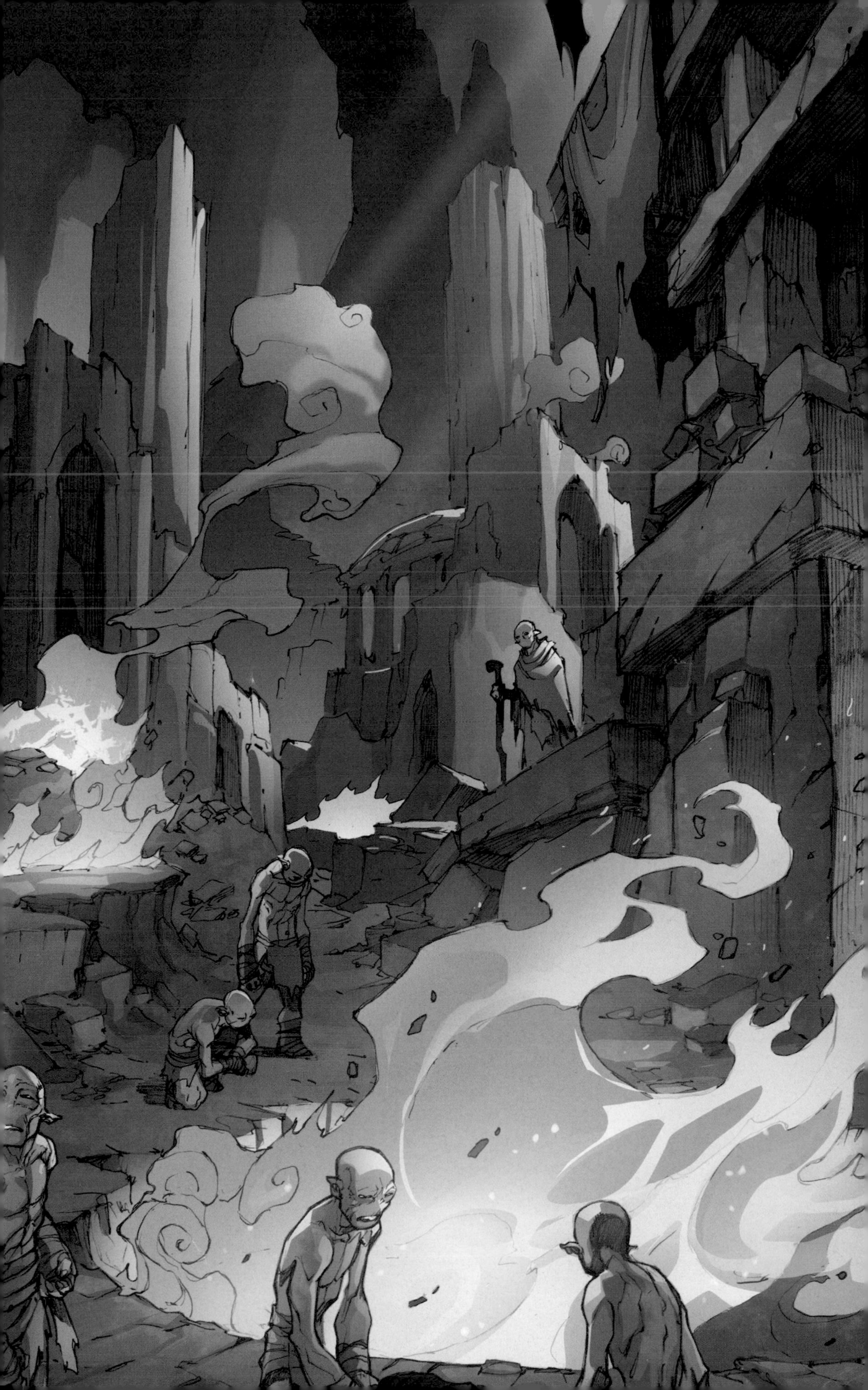

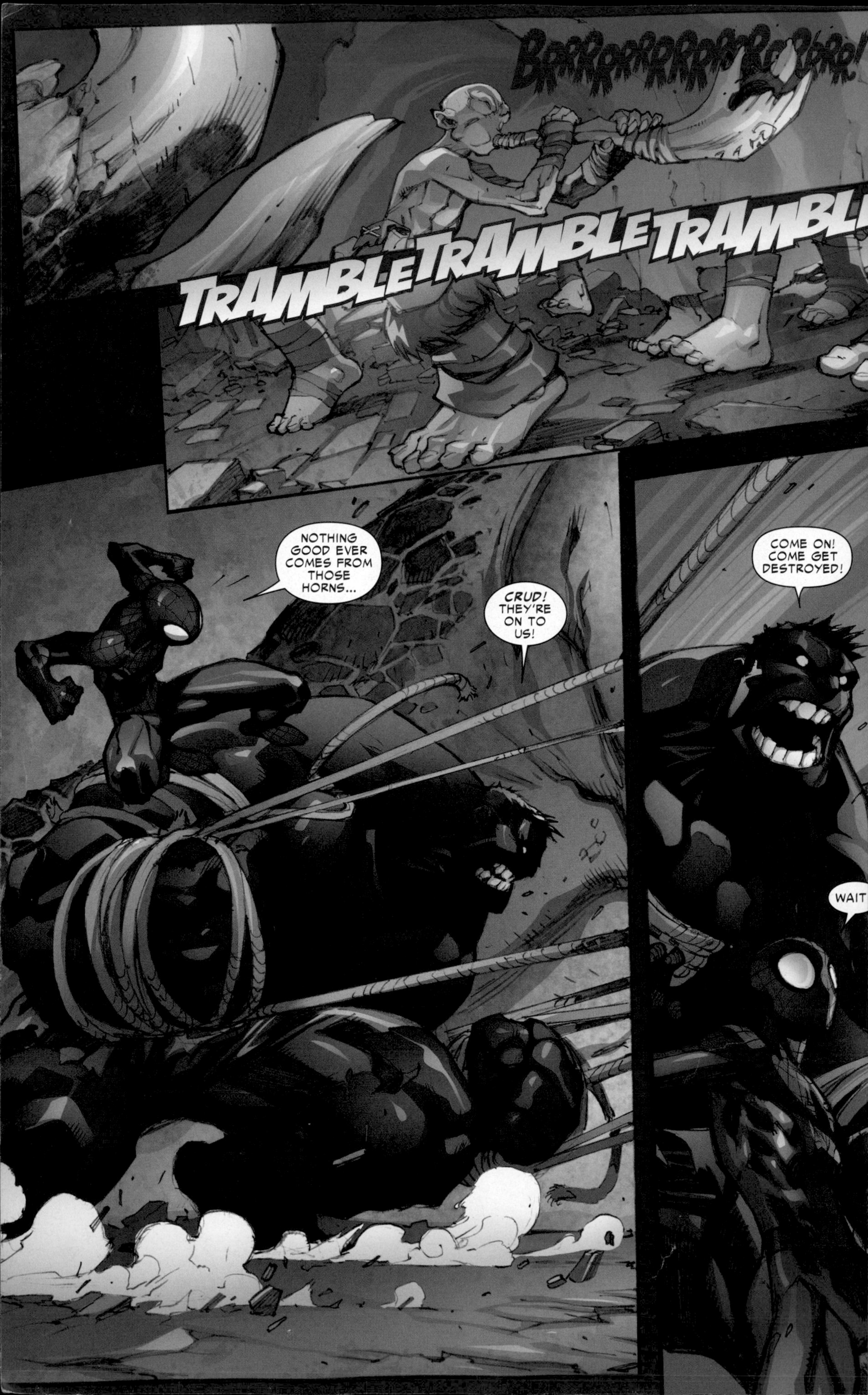
BRRRRRRRRRRRRRRRRR!
TRAMBLE TRAMBLE TRAMBLE
NOTHING GOOD EVER COMES FROM THOSE HORNS...
CRUD! THEY'RE ON TO US!
COME ON! COME GET DESTROYED!
WAIT

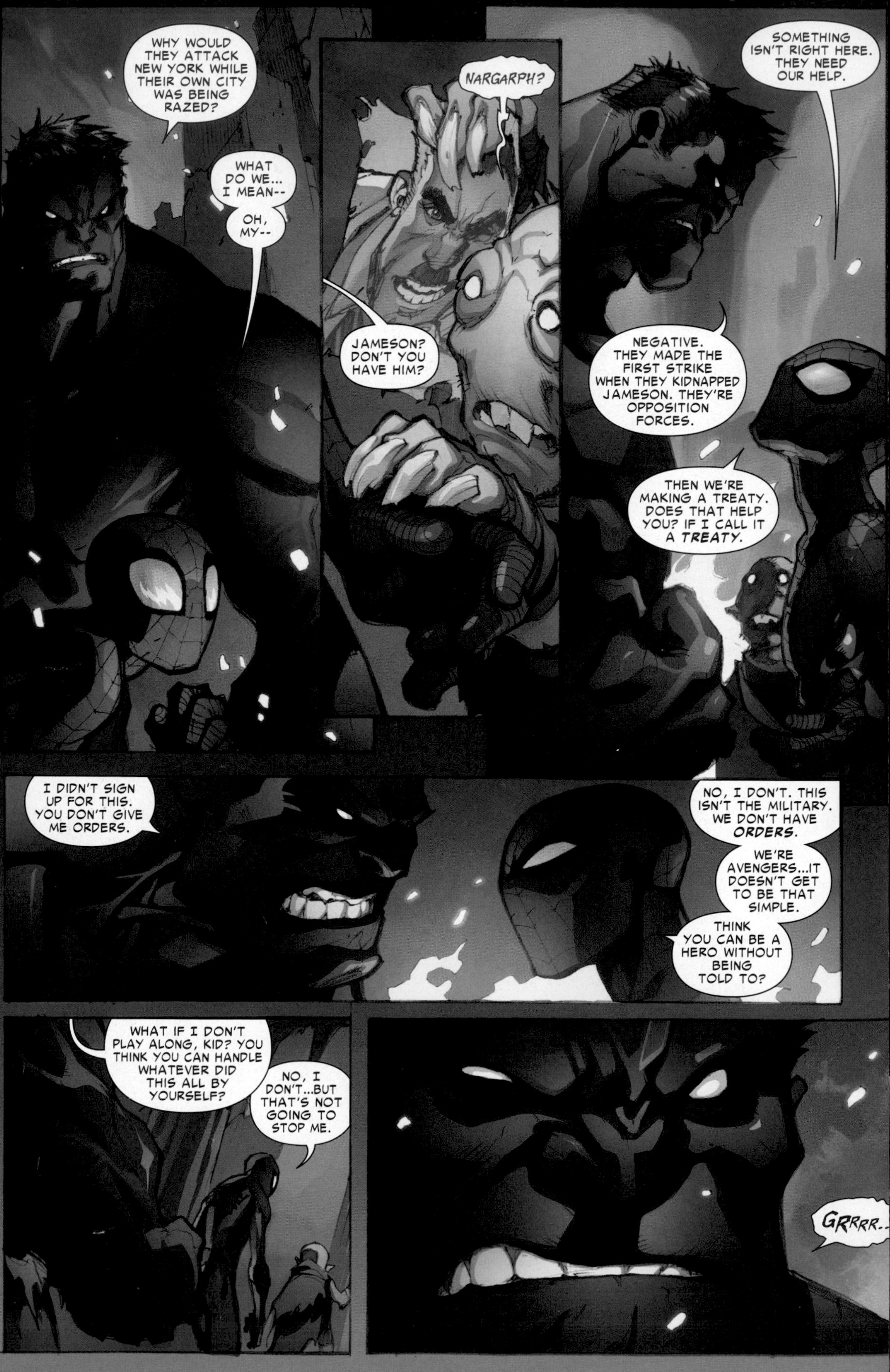
WHY WOULD THEY ATTACK NEW YORK WHILE THEIR OWN CITY WAS BEING RAZED?
WHAT DO WE... I MEAN--
OH, MY--
NARGARPH?
JAMESON? DON'T YOU HAVE HIM?
SOMETHING ISN'T RIGHT HERE. THEY NEED OUR HELP.
NEGATIVE. THEY MADE THE FIRST STRIKE WHEN THEY KIDNAPPED JAMESON. THEY'RE OPPOSITION FORCES.
THEN WE'RE MAKING A TREATY. DOES THAT HELP YOU? IF I CALL IT A TREATY.
I DIDN'T SIGN UP FOR THIS. YOU DON'T GIVE ME ORDERS.
NO, I DON'T. THIS ISN'T THE MILITARY. WE DON'T HAVE ORDERS.
WE'RE AVENGERS...IT DOESN'T GET TO BE THAT SIMPLE.
THINK YOU CAN BE A HERO WITHOUT BEING TOLD TO?
WHAT IF I DON'T PLAY ALONG, KID? YOU THINK YOU CAN HANDLE WHATEVER DID THIS ALL BY YOURSELF?
NO, I DON'T...BUT THAT'S NOT GOING TO STOP ME.
GRRRR...

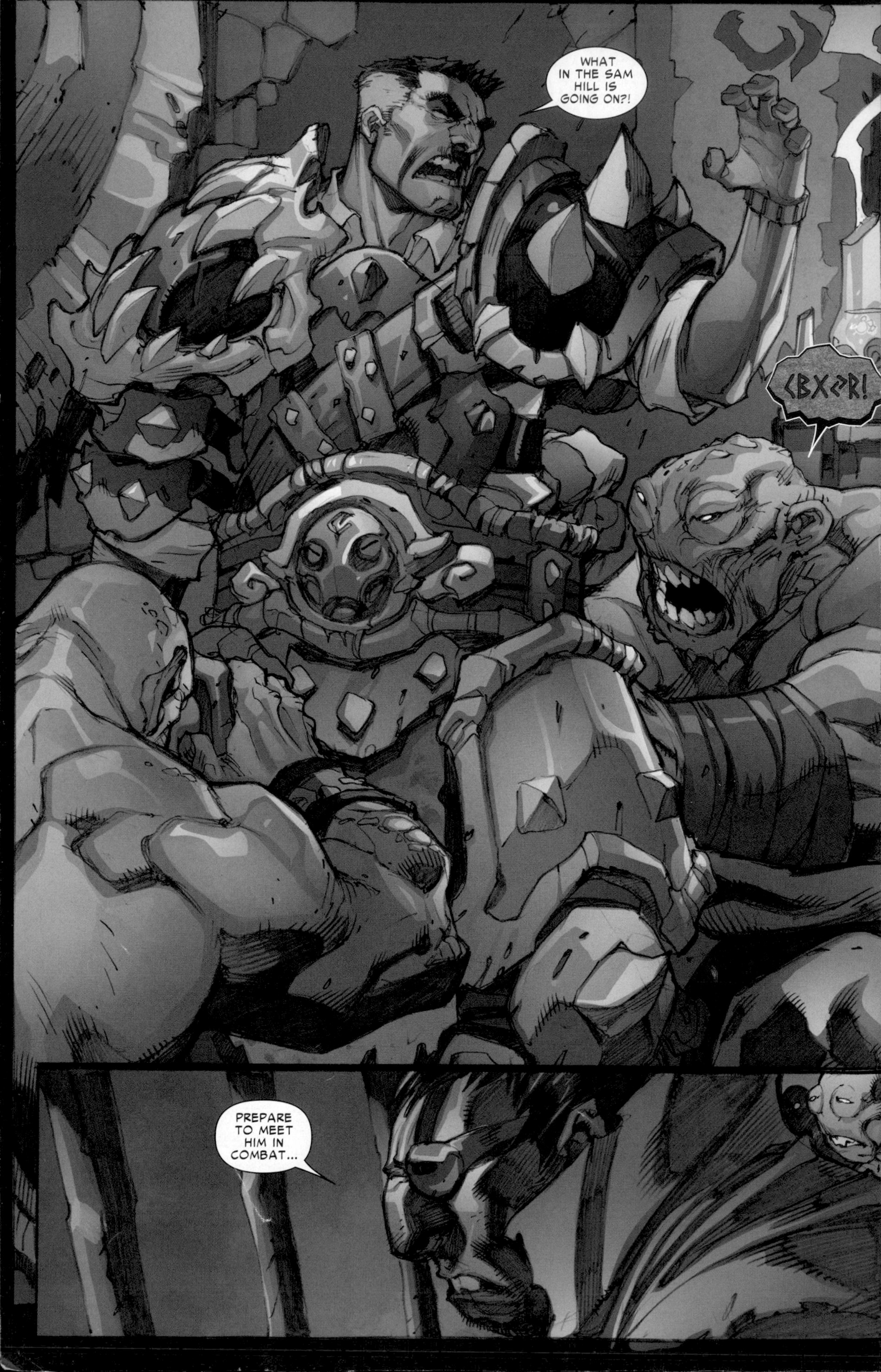
WHAT IN THE SAM HILL IS GOING ON?!
PREPARE TO MEET HIM IN COMBAT...

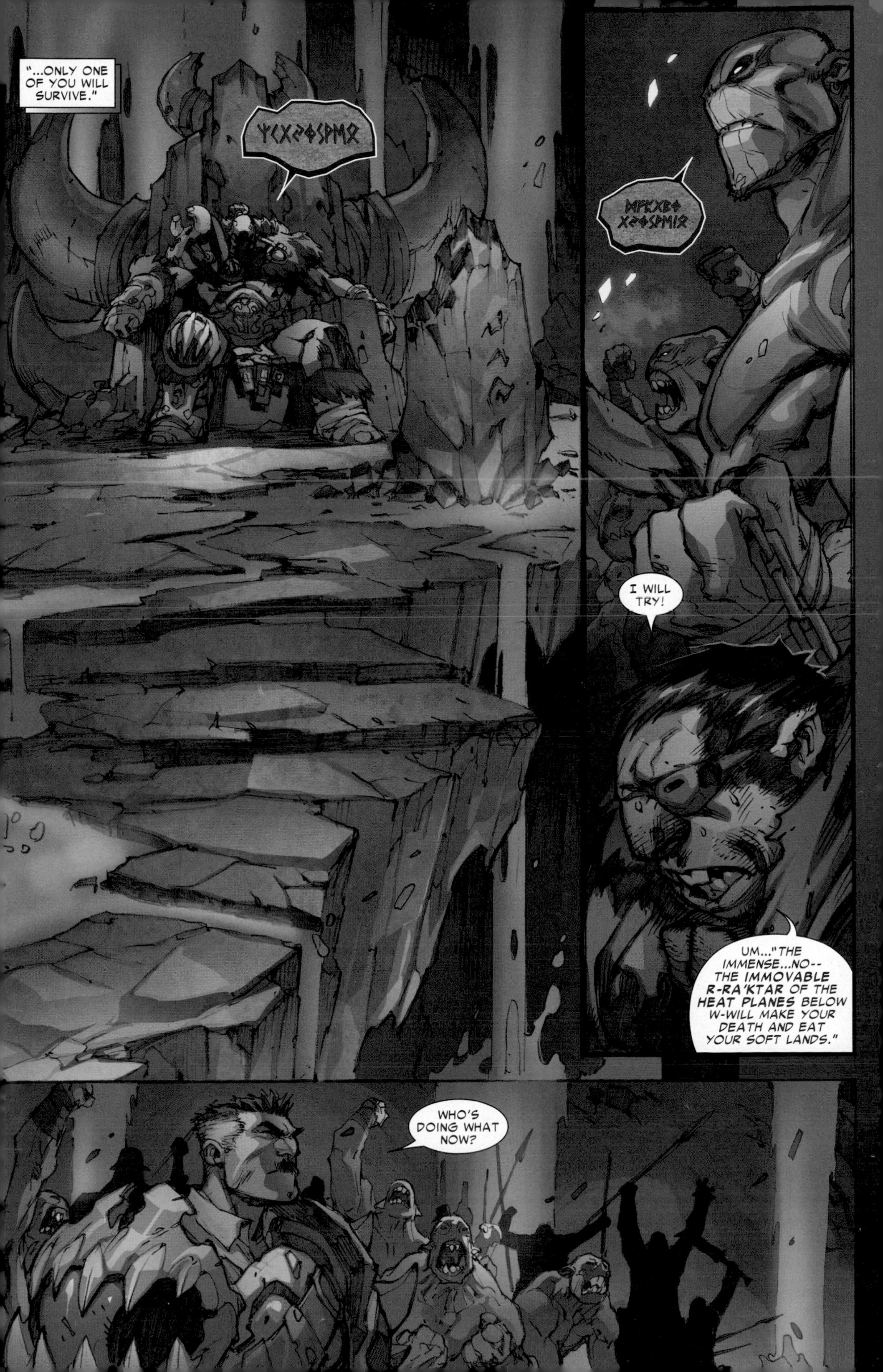
"...ONLY ONE OF YOU WILL SURVIVE."
I WILL TRY!
UM..."THE IMMENSE...NO-- THE **IMMOVABLE R-RA'KTAR** OF THE **HEAT PLANES** BELOW W-WILL MAKE YOUR DEATH AND EAT YOUR SOFT LANDS."
WHO'S DOING WHAT NOW?

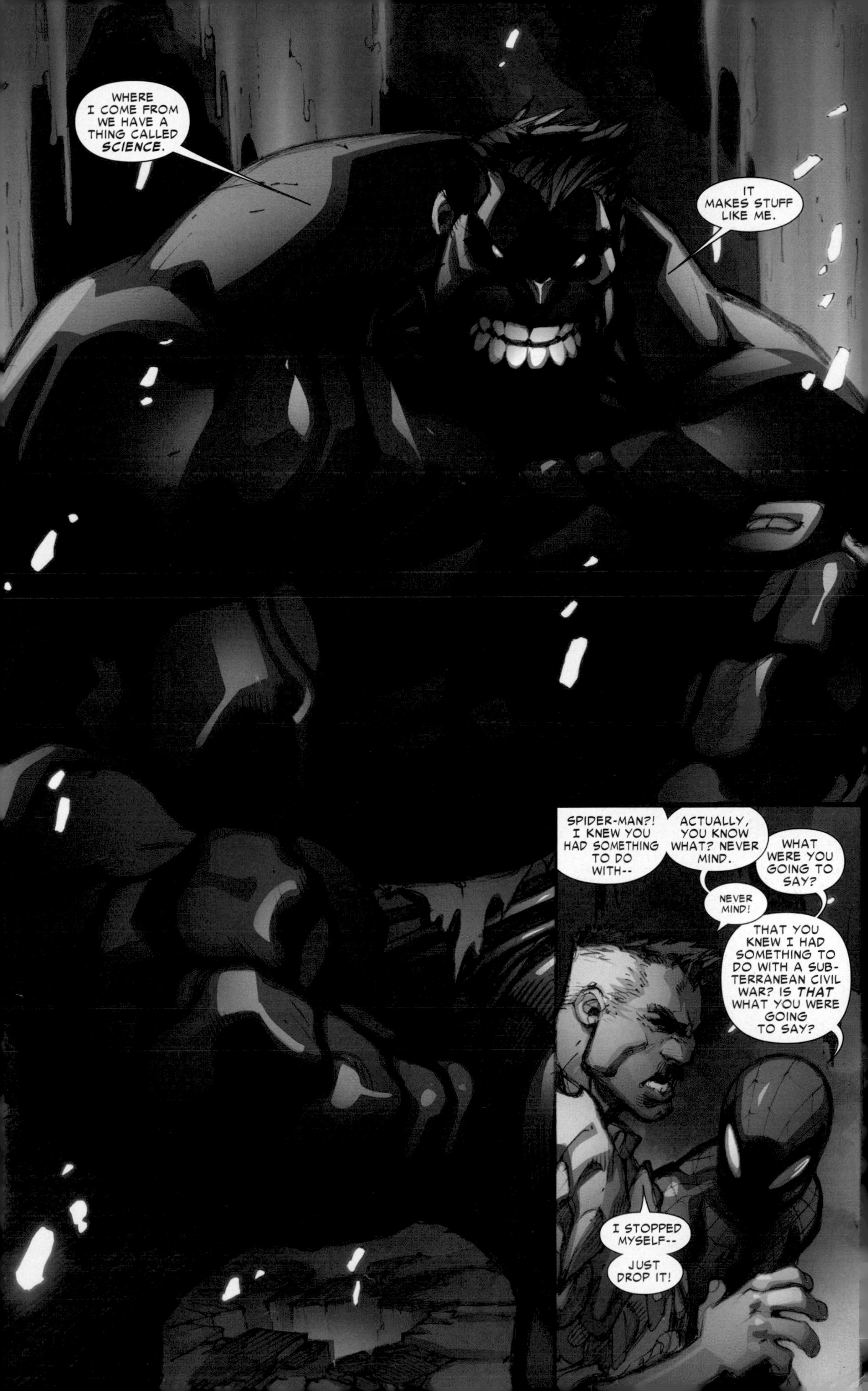
WHERE I COME FROM WE HAVE A THING CALLED *SCIENCE*.
IT MAKES STUFF LIKE ME.
SPIDER-MAN?! I KNEW YOU HAD SOMETHING TO DO WITH--
ACTUALLY, YOU KNOW WHAT? NEVER MIND.
WHAT WERE YOU GOING TO SAY?
NEVER MIND!
THAT YOU KNEW I HAD SOMETHING TO DO WITH A SUB-TERRANEAN CIVIL WAR? IS *THAT* WHAT YOU WERE GOING TO SAY?
I STOPPED MYSELF--
JUST DROP IT!

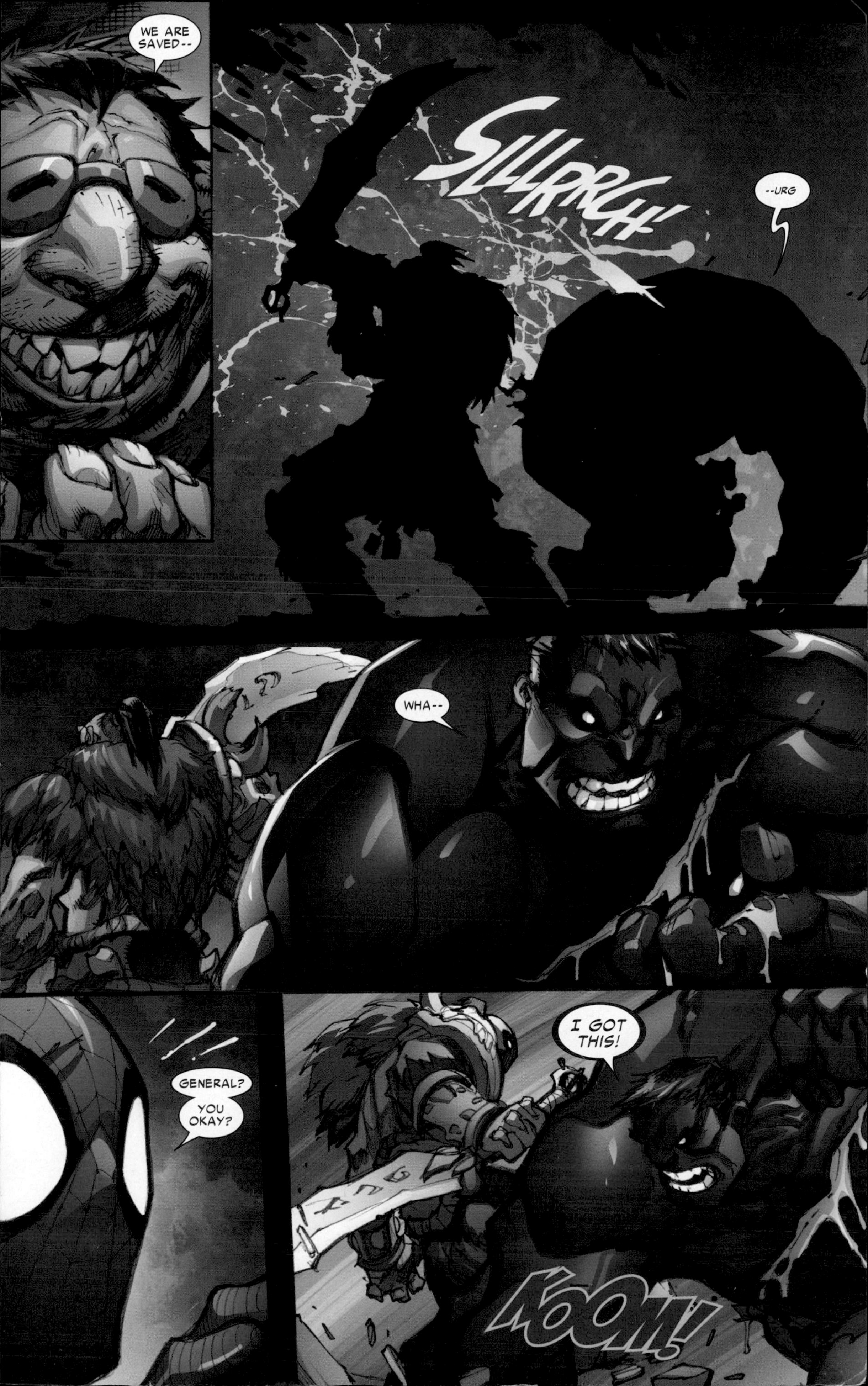
WE ARE SAVED--
SLLRRCH!
--URG
WHA--
!!!
GENERAL? YOU OKAY?
I GOT THIS!
KOOM!

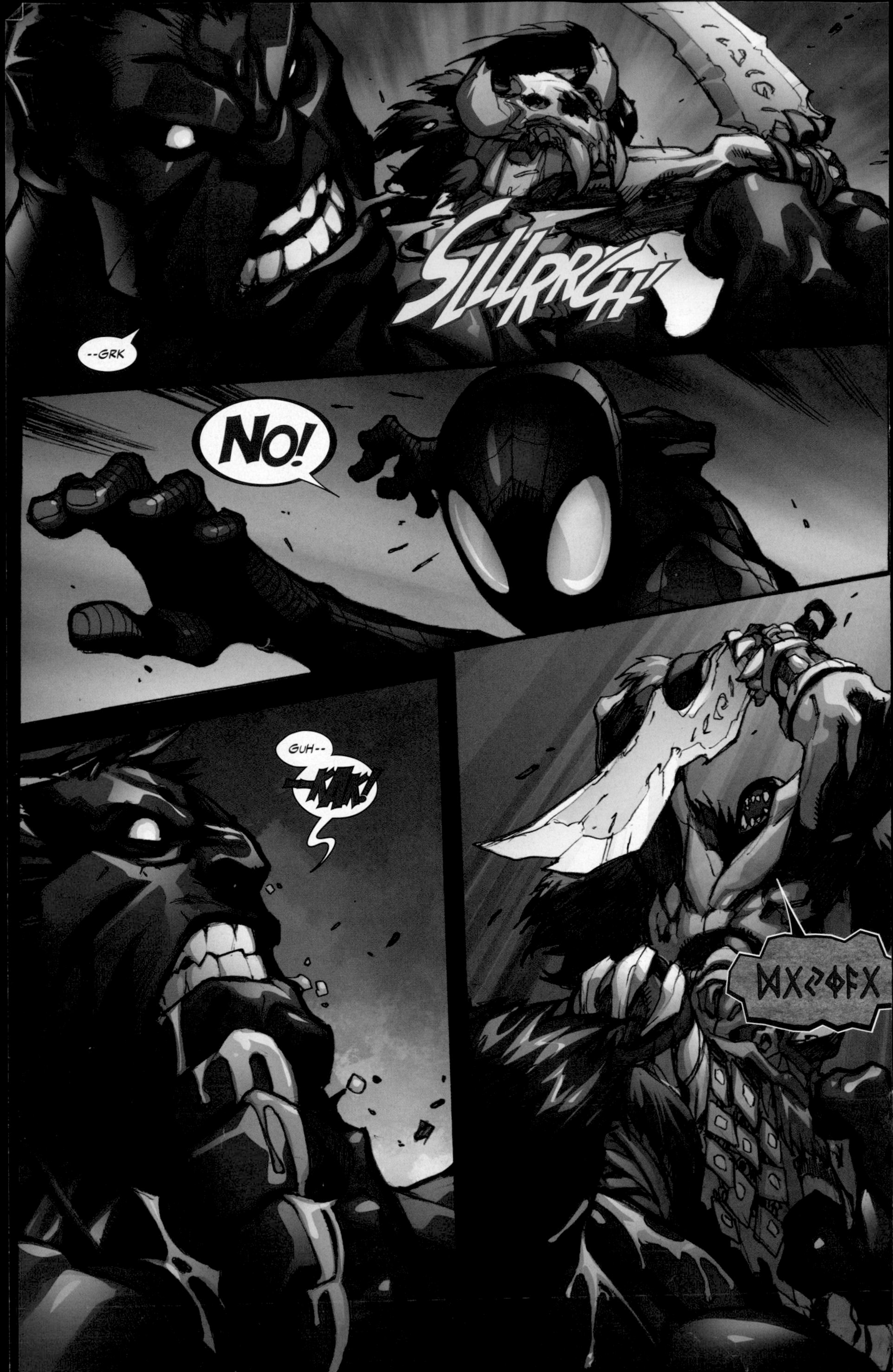
SLLLRRCH!
--GRK
NO!
GUH--
--KIK!
ᛞᚷᚲᛟᚠᚷ

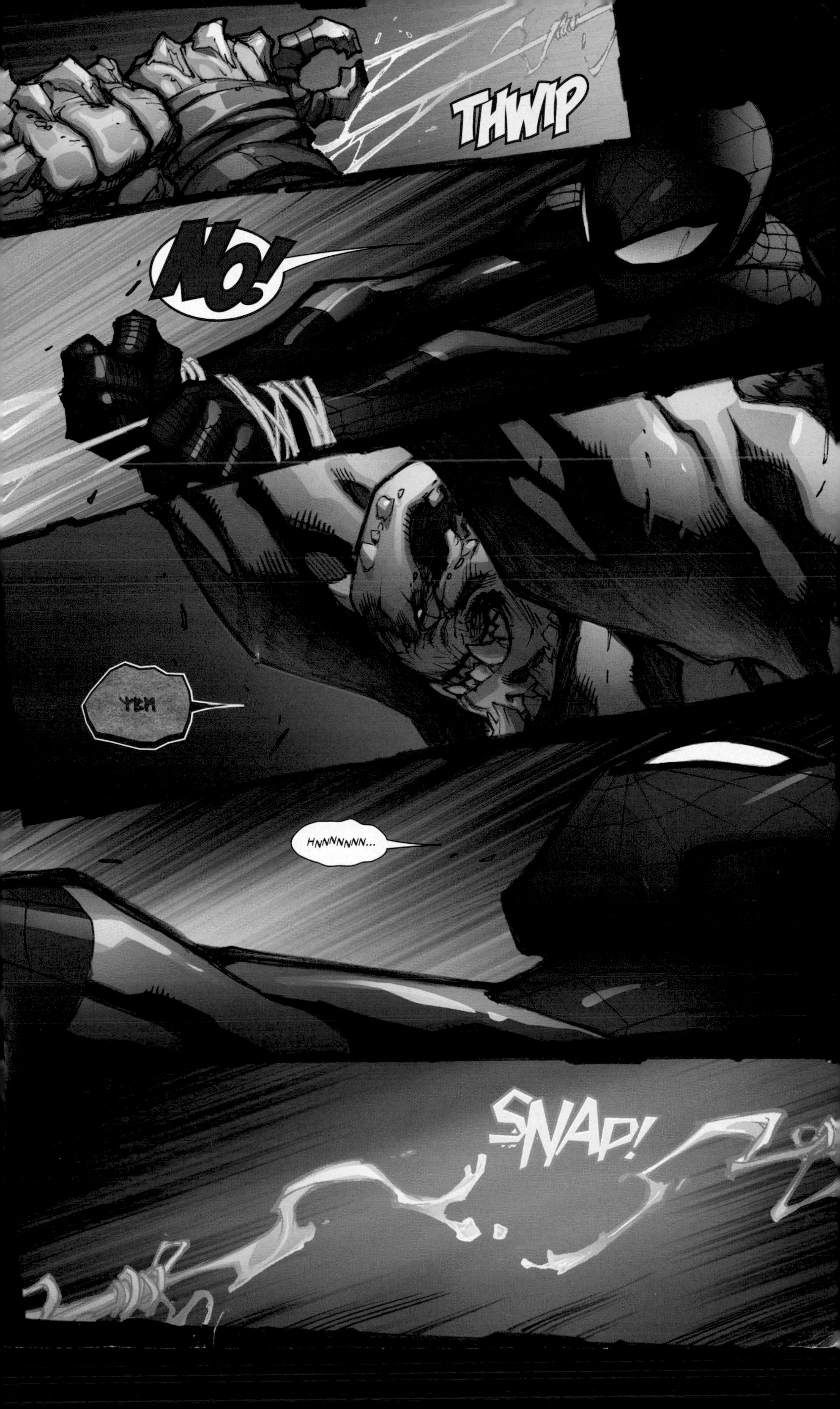
THWIP
NO!
YBM
HNNNNNNN...
SNAP!

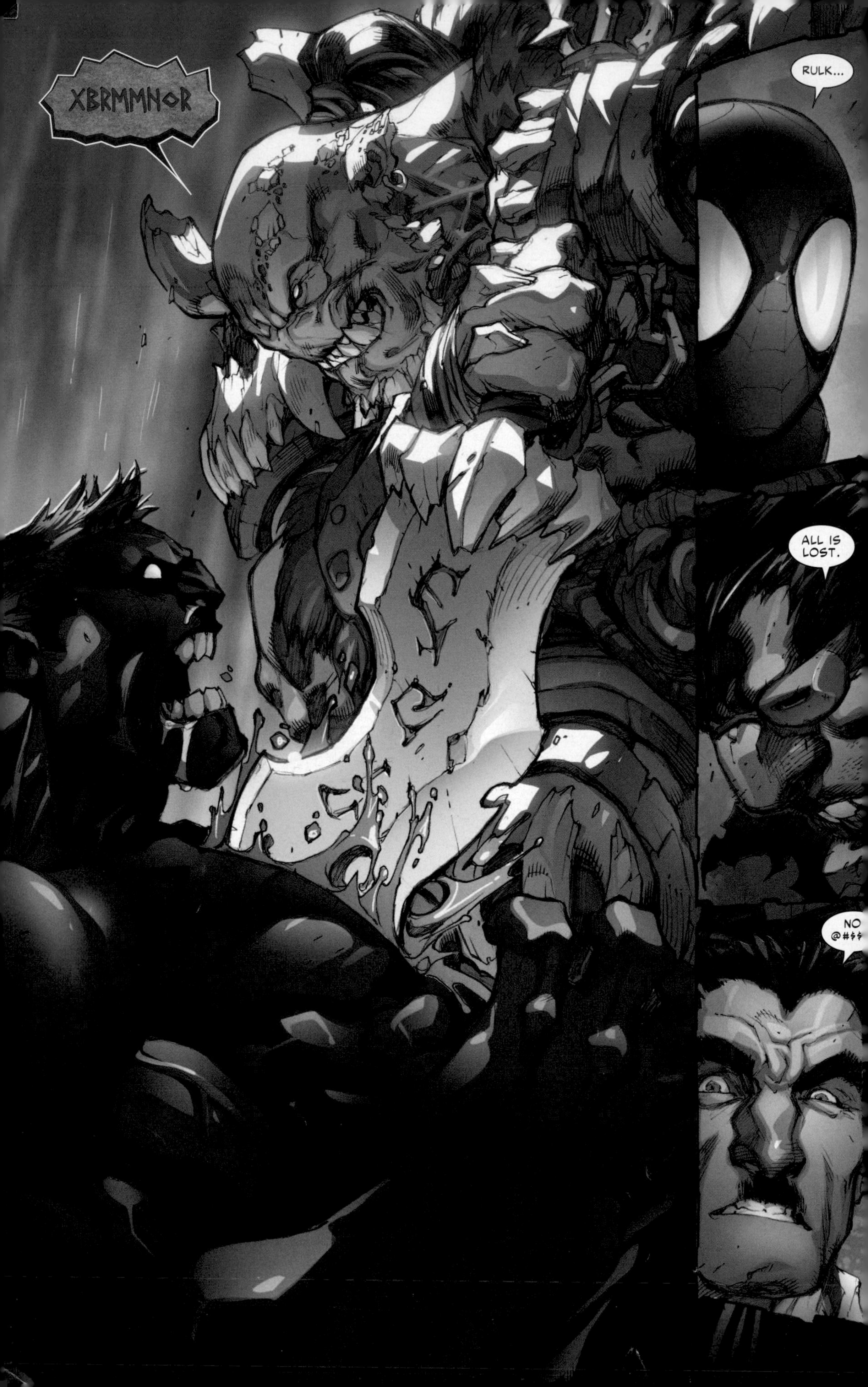
XBRMMNOR
RULK...
ALL IS LOST.
NO @#$$

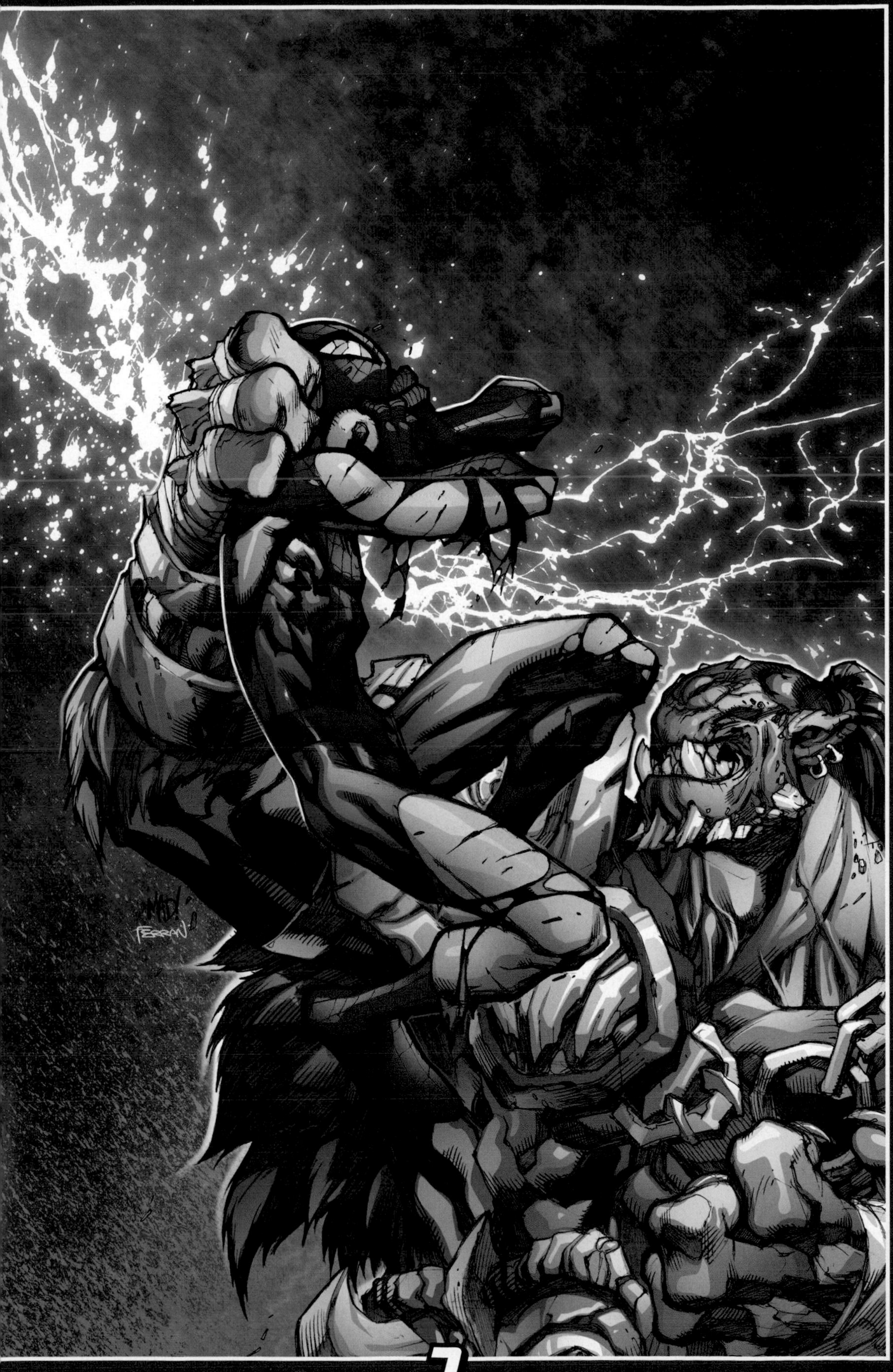

3

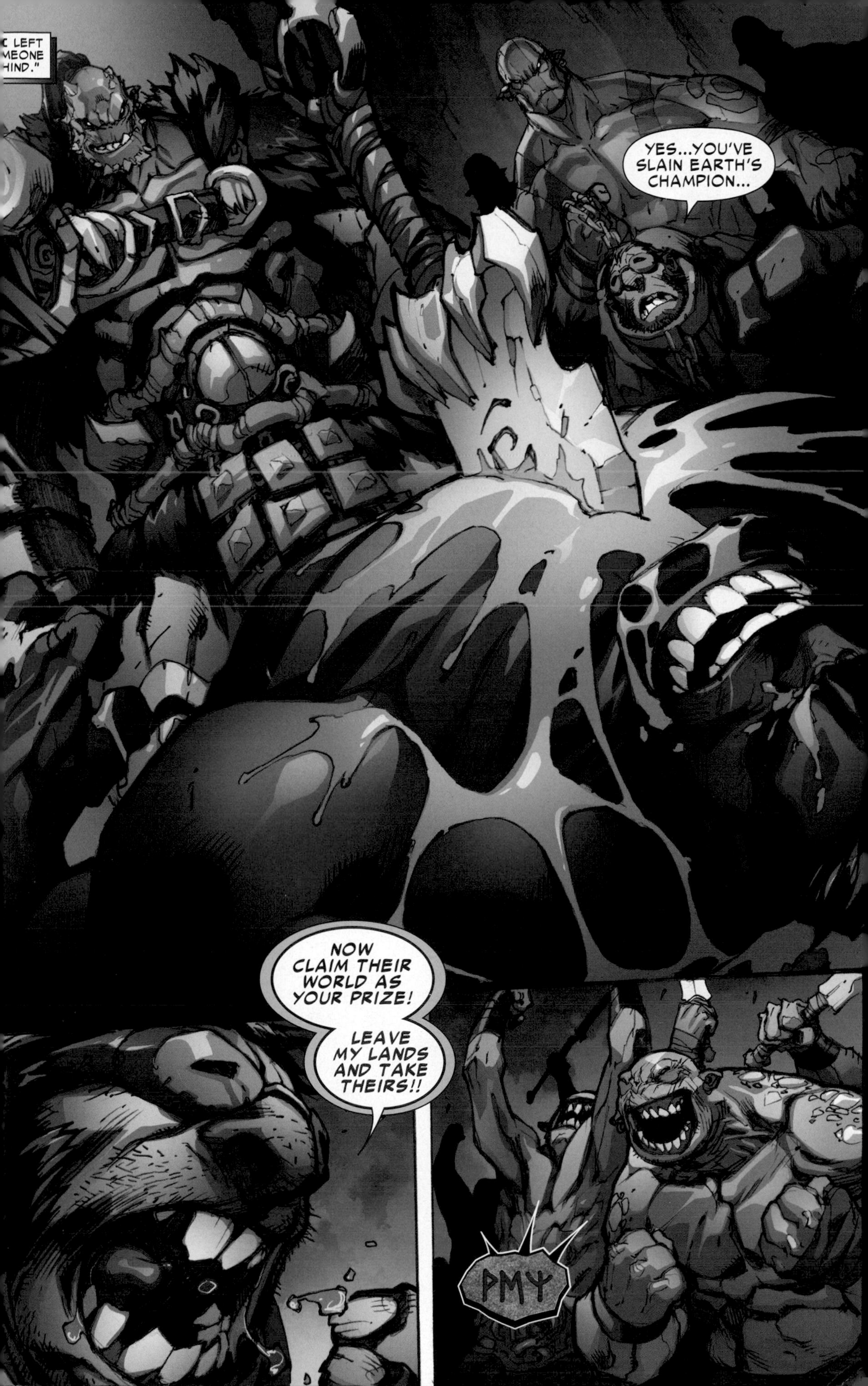

MEONE
HIND."
YES...YOU'VE SLAIN EARTH'S CHAMPION...
NOW CLAIM THEIR WORLD AS YOUR PRIZE!
LEAVE MY LANDS AND TAKE THEIRS!!

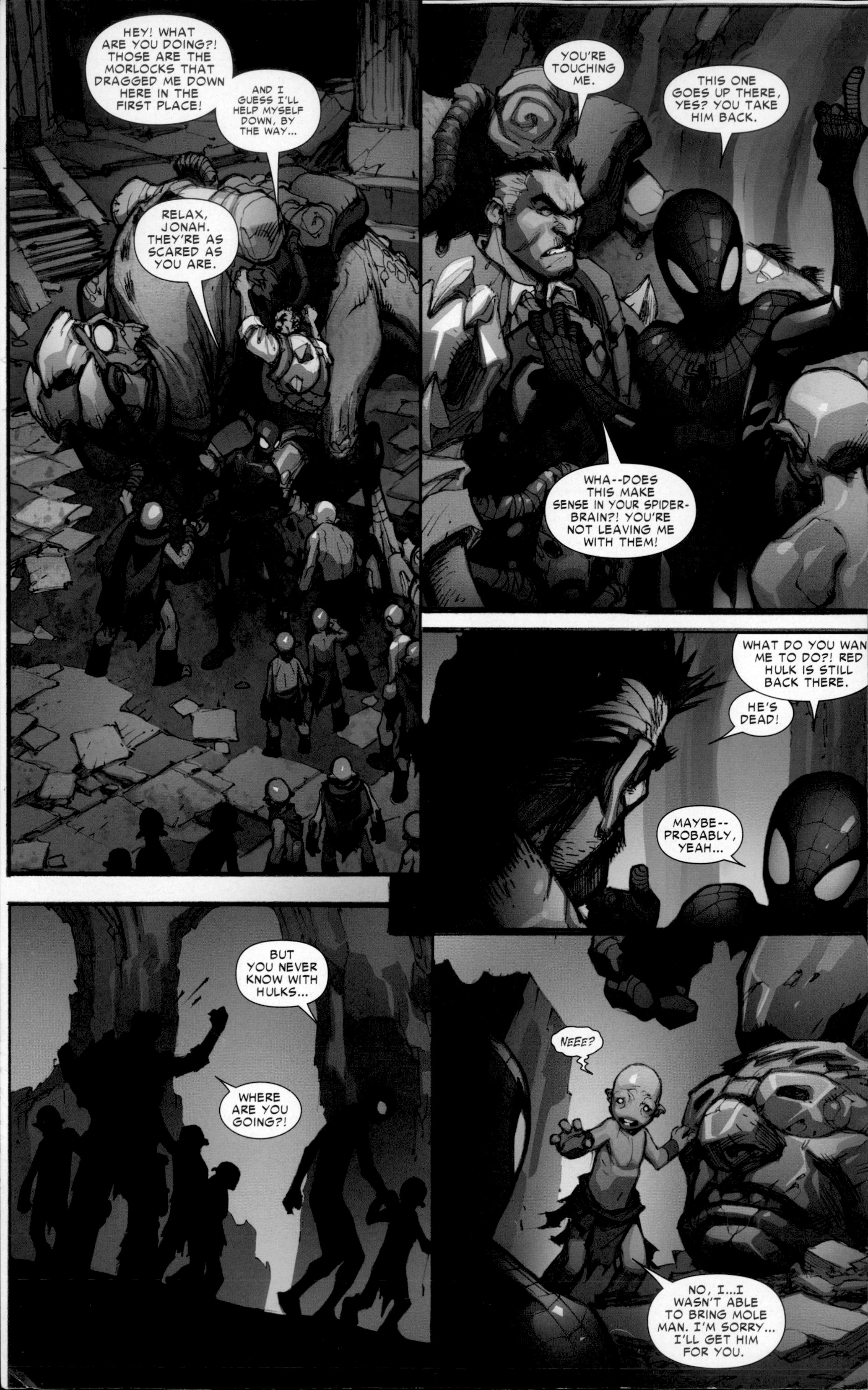
HEY! WHAT ARE YOU DOING?! THOSE ARE THE MORLOCKS THAT DRAGGED ME DOWN HERE IN THE FIRST PLACE!
AND I GUESS I'LL HELP MYSELF DOWN, BY THE WAY...
RELAX, JONAH. THEY'RE AS SCARED AS YOU ARE.
YOU'RE TOUCHING ME.
THIS ONE GOES UP THERE, YES? YOU TAKE HIM BACK.
WHA--DOES THIS MAKE SENSE IN YOUR SPIDER-BRAIN?! YOU'RE NOT LEAVING ME WITH THEM!
WHAT DO YOU WAN ME TO DO?! RED HULK IS STILL BACK THERE.
HE'S DEAD!
MAYBE--PROBABLY, YEAH...
BUT YOU NEVER KNOW WITH HULKS...
WHERE ARE YOU GOING?!
NEEE?
NO, I...I WASN'T ABLE TO BRING MOLE MAN. I'M SORRY... I'LL GET HIM FOR YOU.

THE...*KAFF!* THE AVENGERS ARE...

...ARE GONNA BE REALLY... *HNN...*

...REALLY MAD IF YOU KILL ME.

I'M KIND OF THEIR MASCOT.

ᛑᛉᚠᛂᚠᛗᚱᚠ ᛒᚱᛂᛂᛉᛚᚠᛪᛉ

RA'KTAR REMINDS YOU THAT YOU HAVE NO STAKE TO THESE LANDS. WALK AWAY AND LEAVE HIM TO HIS SLAUGHTER.

PASS.

ᚠᛪᚠ ᚠᛪᚠ

THE GREAT RA'KTAR ASKS IF YOU ARE READY TO DIE...

N-NOT YET... I MEAN...YEAH, IT LOOKS LIKE THAT'S HOW IT'S GOING TO SHAKE OUT, BUT, HEH HEH...

I'VE GOT A FOURTH QUARTER ADDITION TO THE BUCKET LIST.

THWIP!

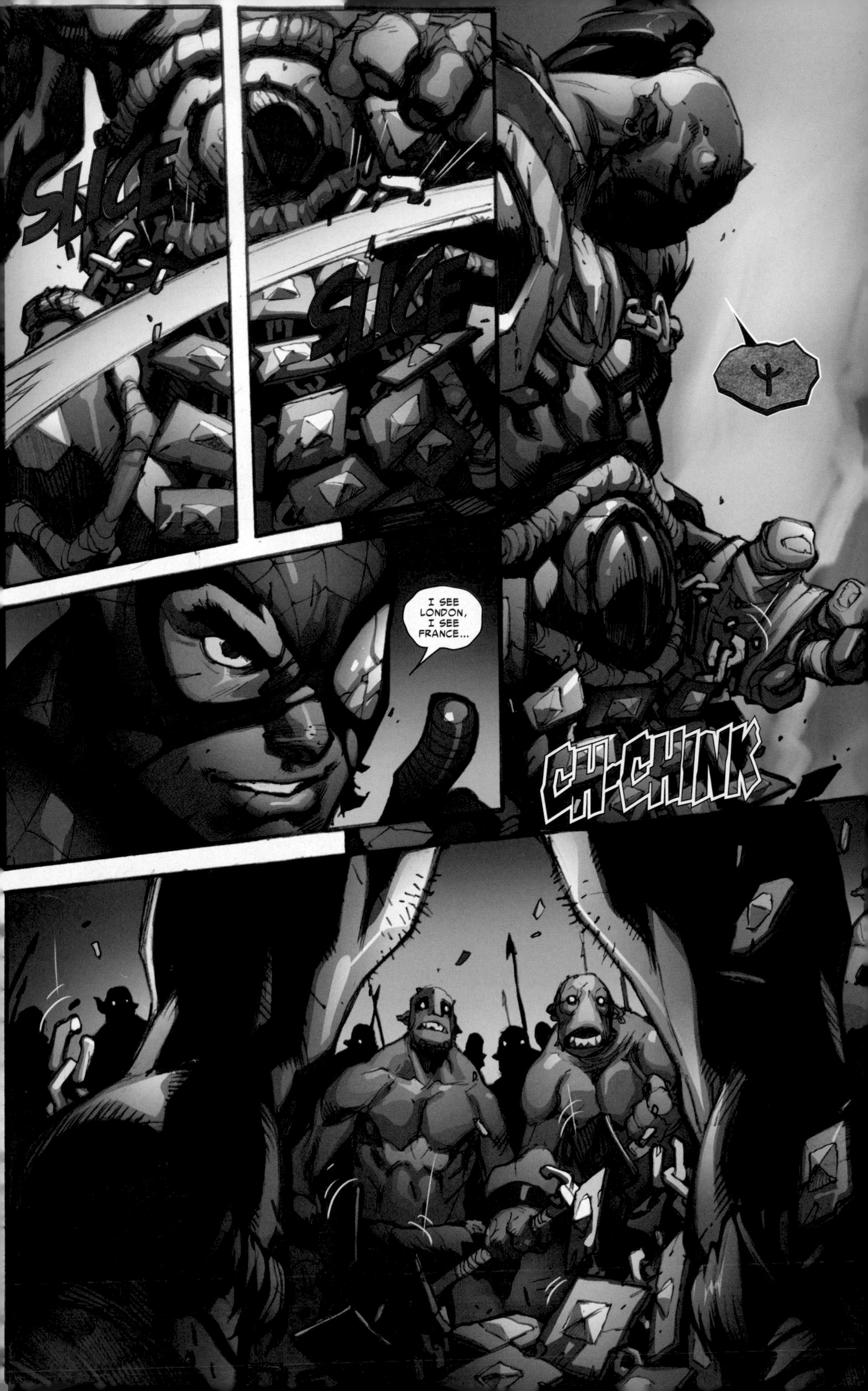
SLICE
SLICE
I SEE LONDON, I SEE FRANCE...
CH-CHINK

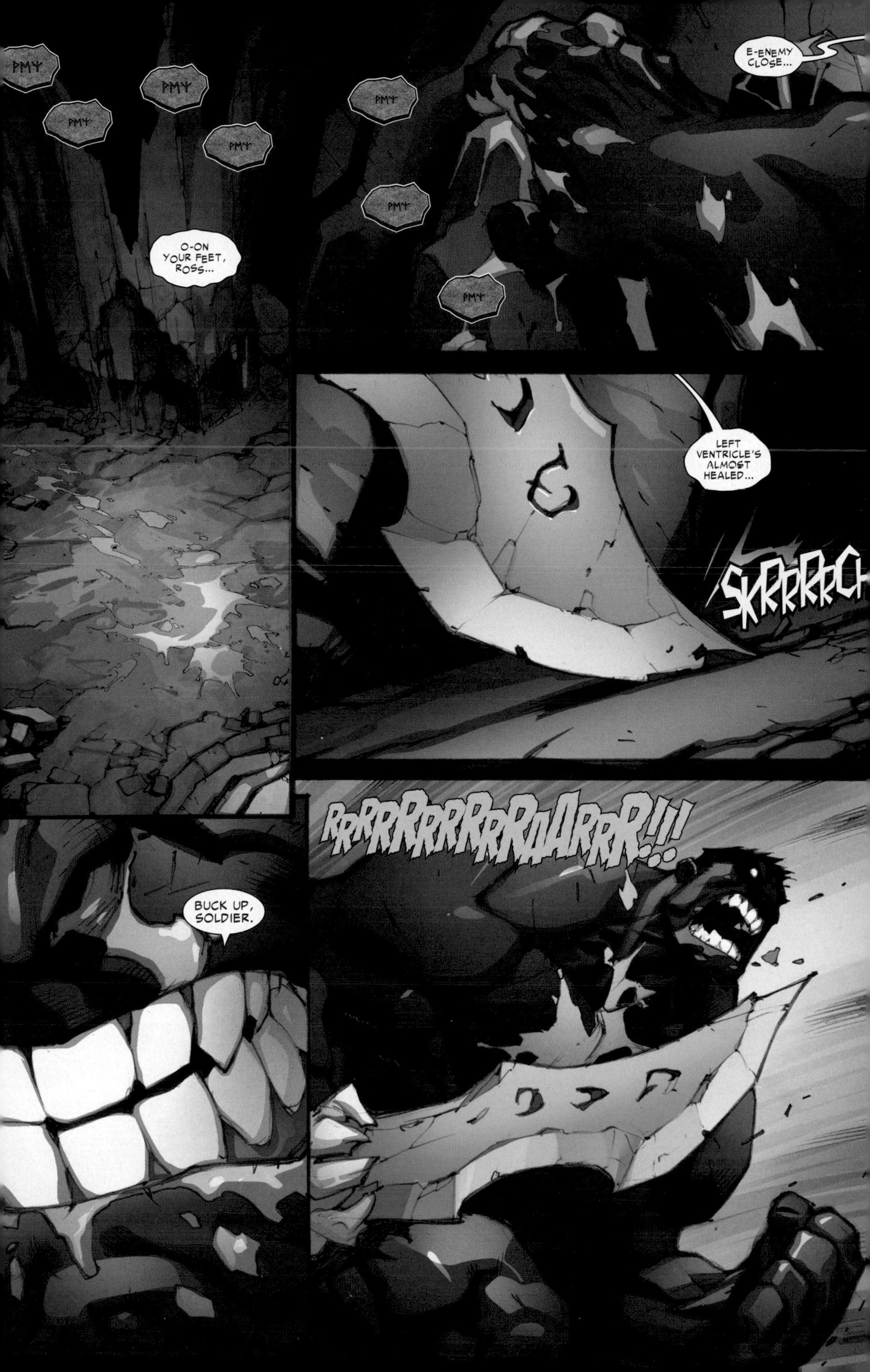
ᚦᛗᛉ
ᚦᛗᛉ
ᚦᛗᛉ
ᚦᛗᛉ
O-ON YOUR FEET, ROSS...
ᚦᛗᛉ
E-ENEMY CLOSE...
ᚦᛗᛉ
ᚦᛗᛉ
LEFT VENTRICLE'S ALMOST HEALED...
SKRRRRRCH
BUCK UP, SOLDIER.
RRRRRRRRRRRAARRR!!!

OOOKAY...

BIO-SCAN'S SHOWING SOME PRETTY EXTENSIVE INJURIES. YOU MIGHT HAVE A CONCUSSION.

NEVER ASK ME FOR A RIDE AGAIN.

HAVE YOU EVER THOUGHT ABOUT A HELMET?

LET'S GET YOU PATCHED UP.

WAIT, WAIT, WAIT! YOU'RE TELLING ME THAT YOU TOOK CARE OF THAT SUBTERRANEAN INVASION WITHOUT THE HULK'S HELP?!

THAT'S RIGHT.

WHAT, WITH YOUR FUNNY LITTLE JOKES?!

YEAH, KIND OF.

--WELL WHAT 'ID YOU DO 'BOUT THE 'MOLE MAN?!

I HELPED HIM OUT OF HIS CHAINS AND LEFT. HE'D SUFFERED ENOUGH.

HE ABDUCTED THE MAYOR OF NEW YORK CITY--NOT TO MENTION THE HUNDREDS OF TIMES HE'S ATTACKED MY CITY!

AND WE'VE ALWAYS REACTED BY PUNCHING HIM IN THE FACE. A LOT.

I THINK WE'RE ALL GONNA BE SURPRISED BY HOW HE REACTS TO A LITTLE KINDNESS.

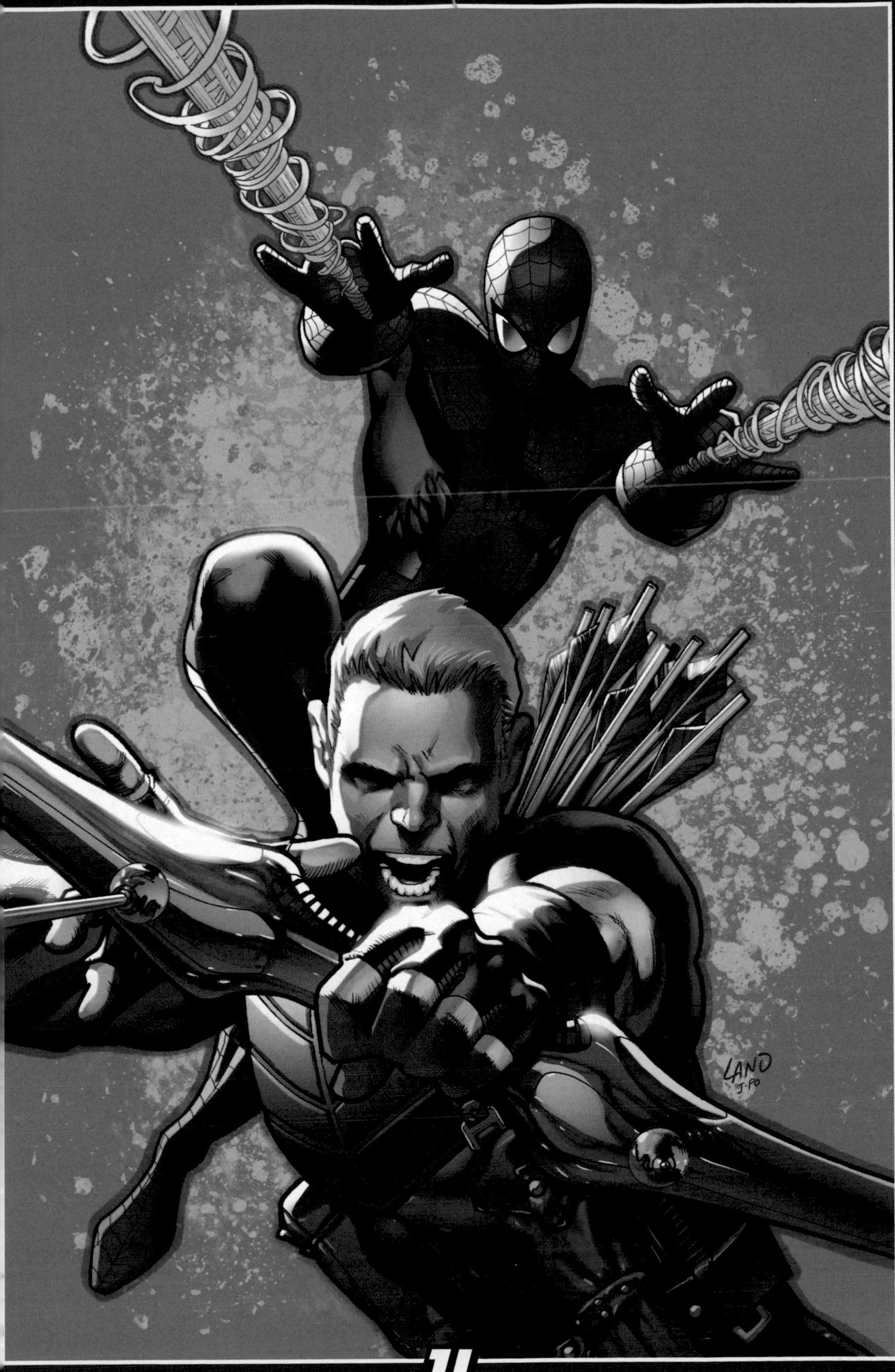
LAND
J-PO

4

While attending a demonstration in radiology, high school student Peter Parker was bitten by a spider which had accidentally been exposed to radioactive rays. Through a miracle of science, Peter soon found that he had gained the spider's powers...and had, in effect become a human spider! Later he joined the Avengers (who have a movie coming out soon).

AVENGING
SPIDER-MAN

After attending a demonstration in radiology, orphan Clint Barton was shot by a radioactive arrow and frozen in World War Two ice where he stayed until he was defrosted by Amazon Warriors during the super hero CIVIL WAR. Soon a hawk bit him in the eye and thus was born...

HAWKEYE*

AVENGING
SPIDER-MAN

WRITER: **ZEB WELLS**   ARTIST: **GREG LAND**

INKER: **JAY LEISTEN**   COLOR ART: **WIL QUINTANA**

LETTERER: **VC's JOE CARAMAGNA**   COVER: **GREG LAND & JUSTIN PONSOR**

VARIANT COVER: **DALE KEOWN & PETER STEIGERWALD**

ASSISTANT EDITOR: **ELLIE PYLE**   EDITOR: **STEPHEN WACKER**

EXECUTIVE EDITOR: **TOM BREVOORT**   EDITOR IN CHIEF: **AXEL ALONSO**

CHIEF CREATIVE OFFICER: **JOE QUESADA**   PUBLISHER: **DAN BUCKLEY**   EXECUTIVE PRODUCER: **ALAN FINE**

*Sorry, folks. Wacker's an idiot who doesn't do a lot of research. ACTUALLY Clint Barton was orphaned at an early age and ran away to join the circus where he was trained to be an expert archer. While initially following a life of petty crime, Clint was inspired by the heroism of Iron Man to prove his skills to Earth's Mightiest Heroes and has become one of their most legendary members. How Wacker cannot know all this at this stage in his "career" is beyond me. -Zeb

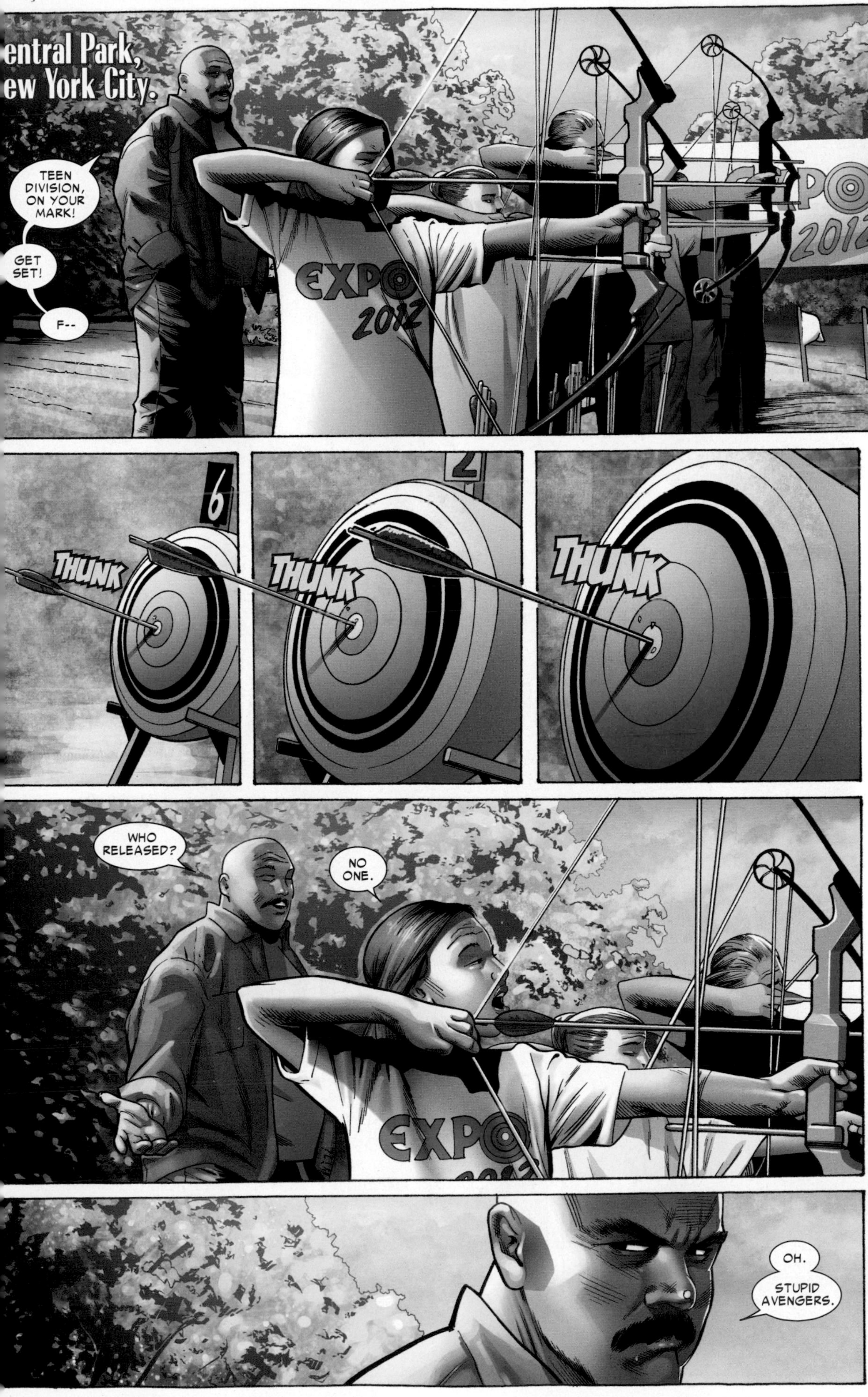
entral Park,
ew York City.
TEEN DIVISION, ON YOUR MARK!
GET SET!
F--
EXPO 2012
THUNK
THUNK
THUNK
WHO RELEASED?
NO ONE.
OH.
STUPID AVENGERS.

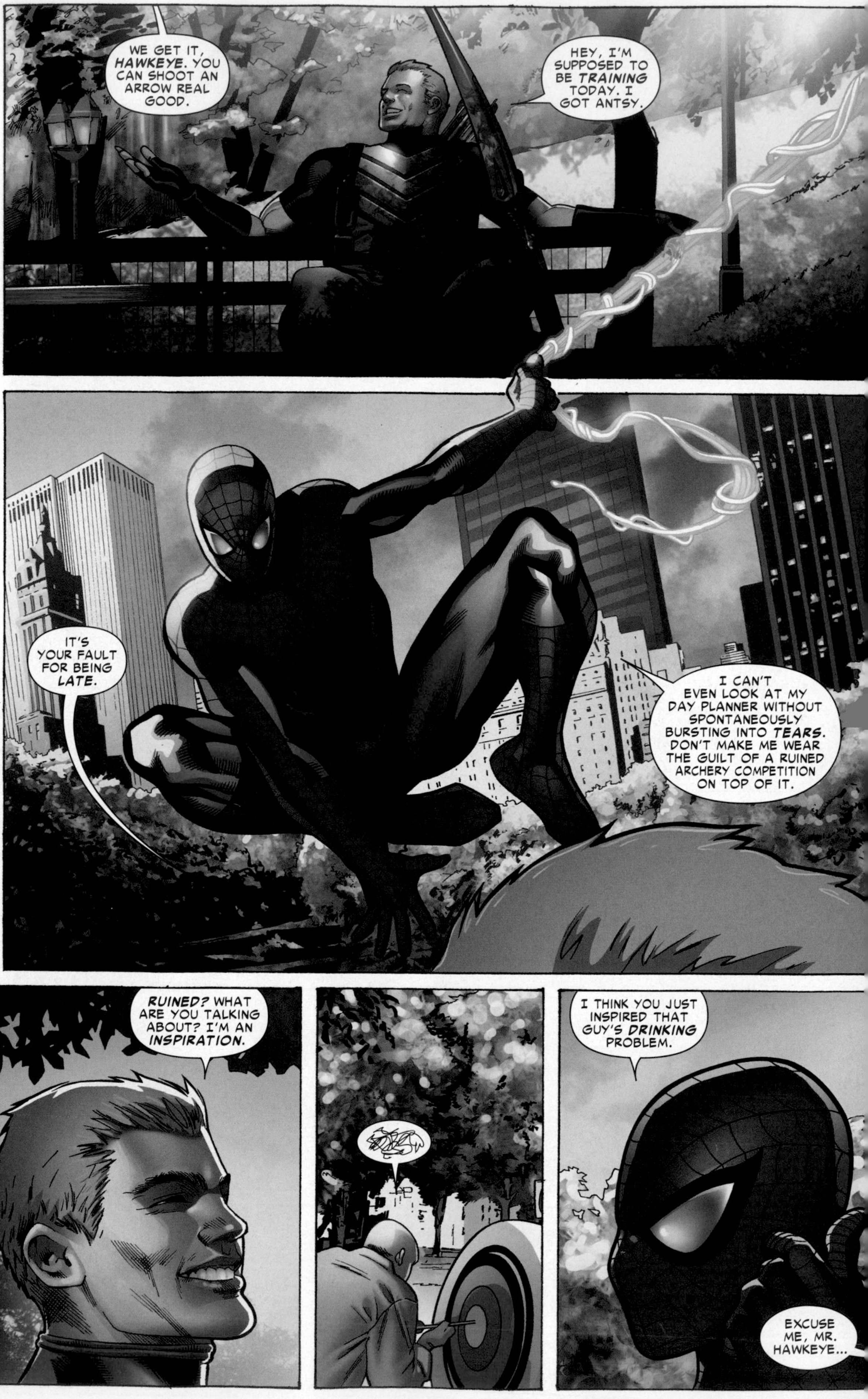
WE GET IT, HAWKEYE. YOU CAN SHOOT AN ARROW REAL GOOD.
HEY, I'M SUPPOSED TO BE TRAINING TODAY. I GOT ANTSY.
IT'S YOUR FAULT FOR BEING LATE.
I CAN'T EVEN LOOK AT MY DAY PLANNER WITHOUT SPONTANEOUSLY BURSTING INTO TEARS. DON'T MAKE ME WEAR THE GUILT OF A RUINED ARCHERY COMPETITION ON TOP OF IT.
RUINED? WHAT ARE YOU TALKING ABOUT? I'M AN INSPIRATION.
I THINK YOU JUST INSPIRED THAT GUY'S DRINKING PROBLEM.
EXCUSE ME, MR. HAWKEYE...

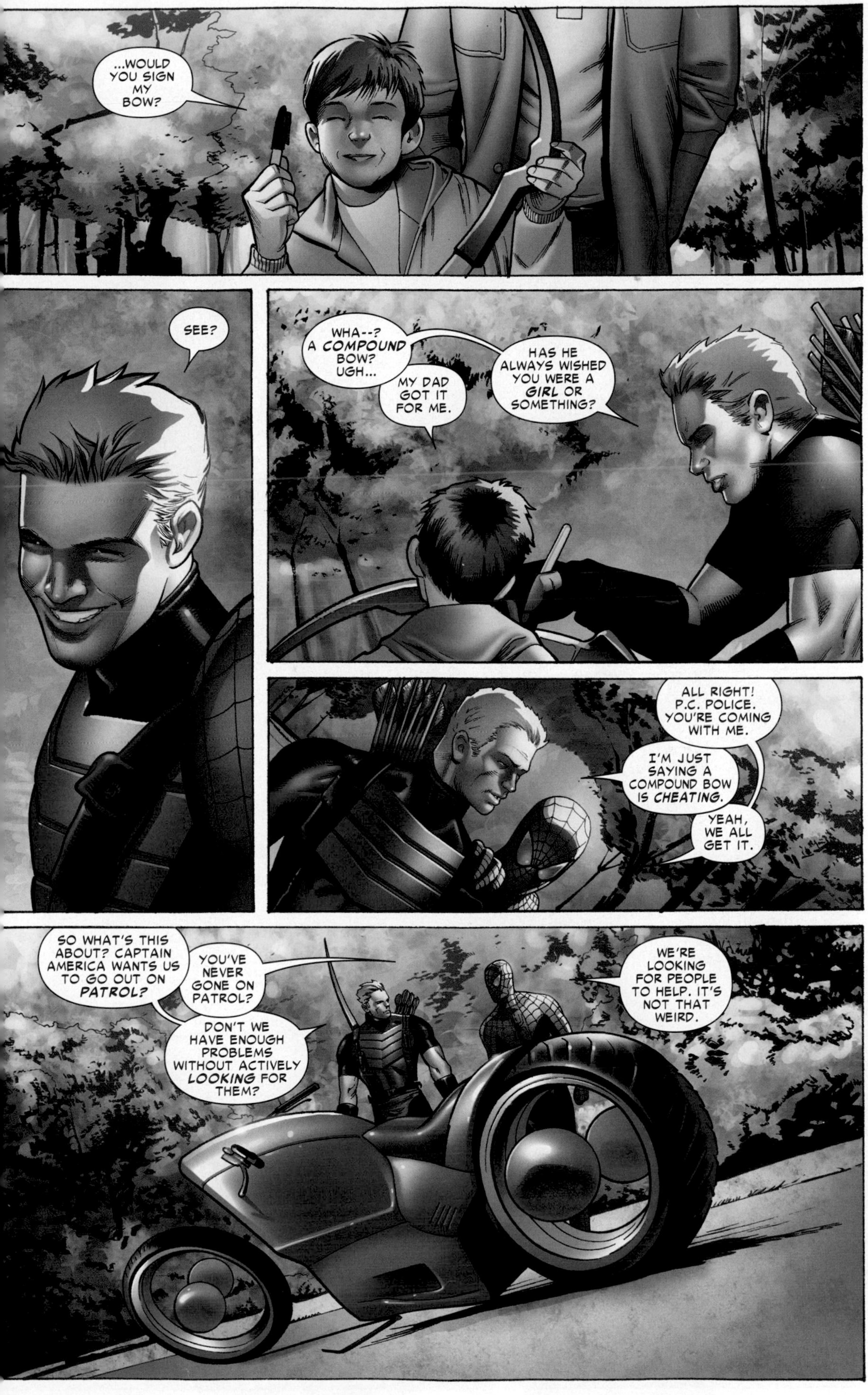
...WOULD YOU SIGN MY BOW?
SEE?
WHA--? A COMPOUND BOW? UGH...
MY DAD GOT IT FOR ME.
HAS HE ALWAYS WISHED YOU WERE A GIRL OR SOMETHING?
ALL RIGHT! P.C. POLICE. YOU'RE COMING WITH ME.
I'M JUST SAYING A COMPOUND BOW IS CHEATING.
YEAH, WE ALL GET IT.
SO WHAT'S THIS ABOUT? CAPTAIN AMERICA WANTS US TO GO OUT ON PATROL?
YOU'VE NEVER GONE ON PATROL?
DON'T WE HAVE ENOUGH PROBLEMS WITHOUT ACTIVELY LOOKING FOR THEM?
WE'RE LOOKING FOR PEOPLE TO HELP. IT'S NOT THAT WEIRD.

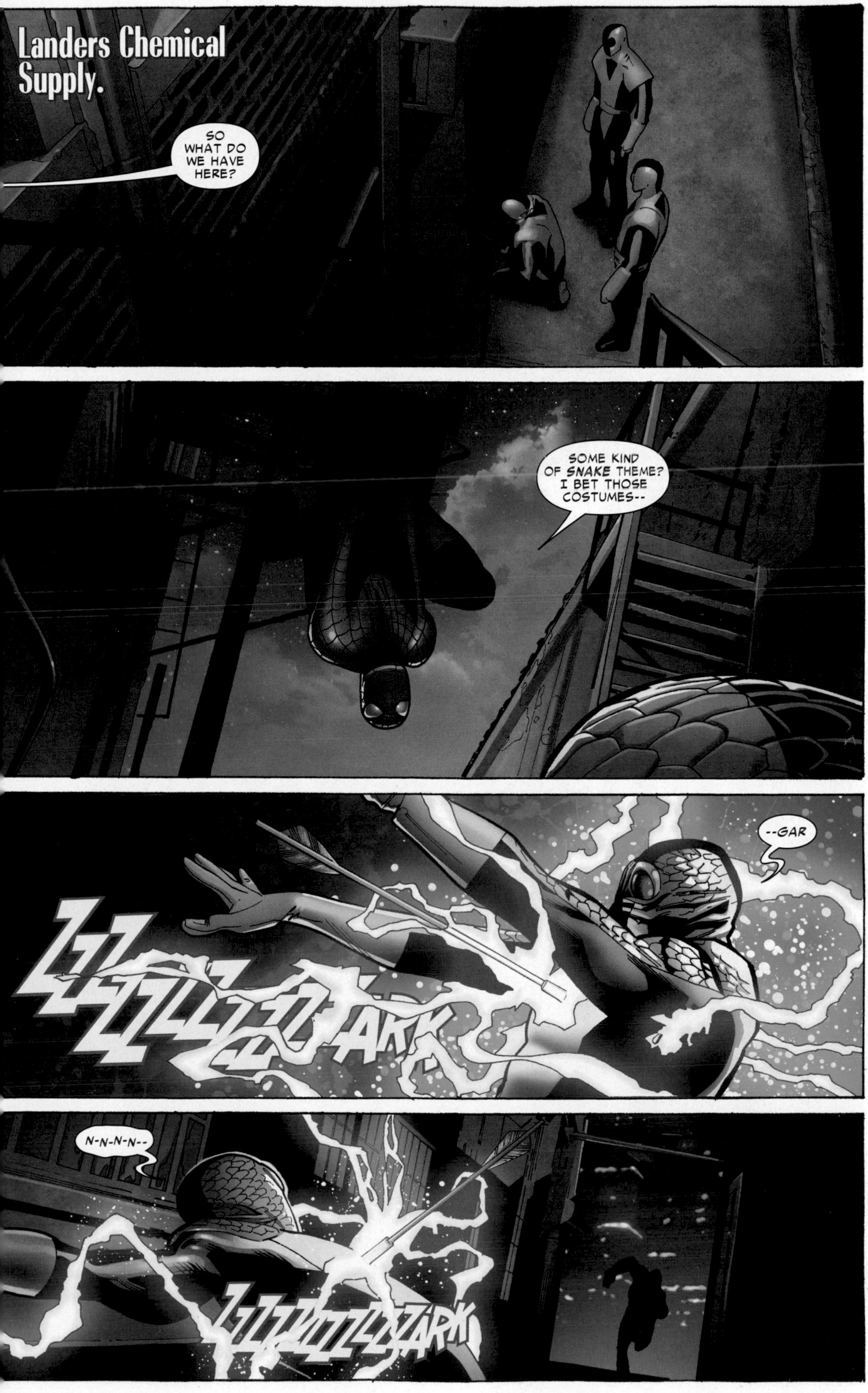
Landers Chemical Supply.
SO WHAT DO WE HAVE HERE?
SOME KIND OF SNAKE THEME? I BET THOSE COSTUMES--
--GAR
ZZZZZZZAK ZARK
N-N-N-N--
ZZZZZZZZZARK

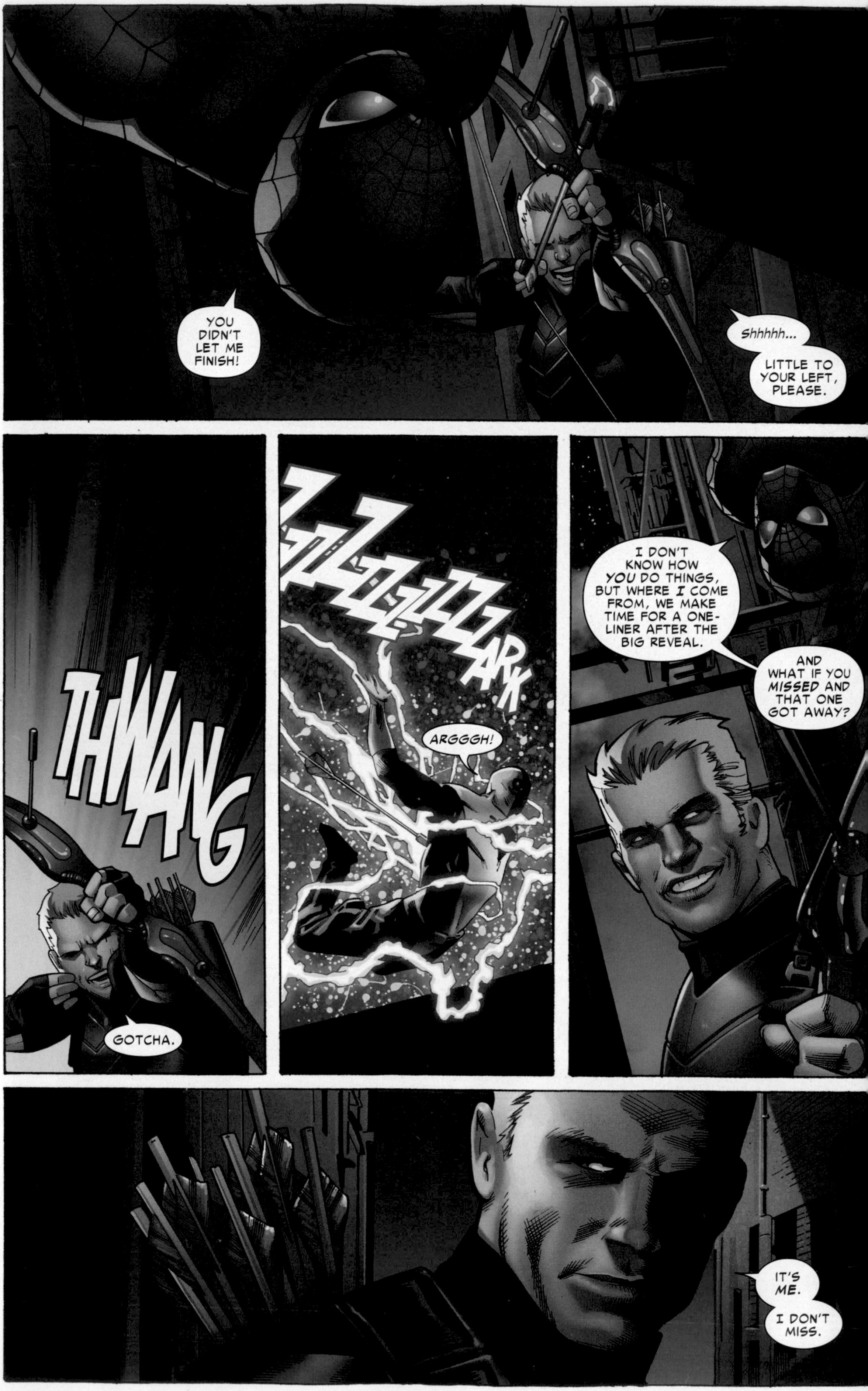
YOU DIDN'T LET ME FINISH!
Shhhhh...
LITTLE TO YOUR LEFT, PLEASE.
THWANG
GOTCHA.
ZZZZZZZZZARK
ARGGGH!
I DON'T KNOW HOW YOU DO THINGS, BUT WHERE I COME FROM, WE MAKE TIME FOR A ONE-LINER AFTER THE BIG REVEAL.
AND WHAT IF YOU MISSED AND THAT ONE GOT AWAY?
IT'S ME.
I DON'T MISS.

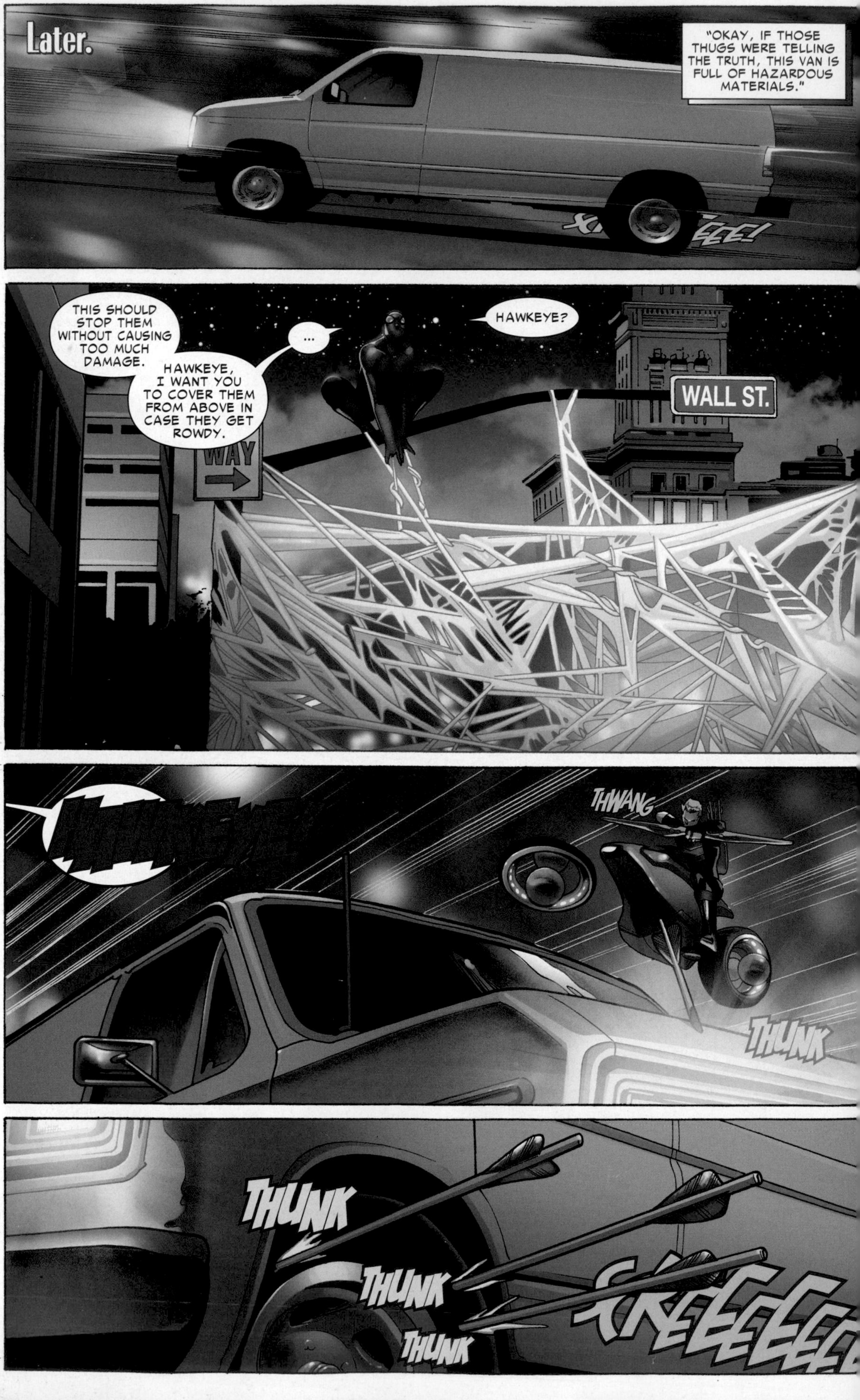
Later.
"OKAY, IF THOSE THUGS WERE TELLING THE TRUTH, THIS VAN IS FULL OF HAZARDOUS MATERIALS."
THIS SHOULD STOP THEM WITHOUT CAUSING TOO MUCH DAMAGE.
HAWKEYE, I WANT YOU TO COVER THEM FROM ABOVE IN CASE THEY GET ROWDY.
...
HAWKEYE?
WALL ST.
WAY
THWANG
THUNK
THUNK
THUNK
THUNK

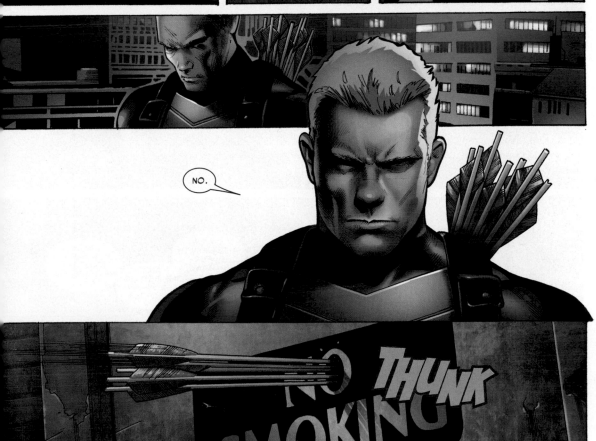

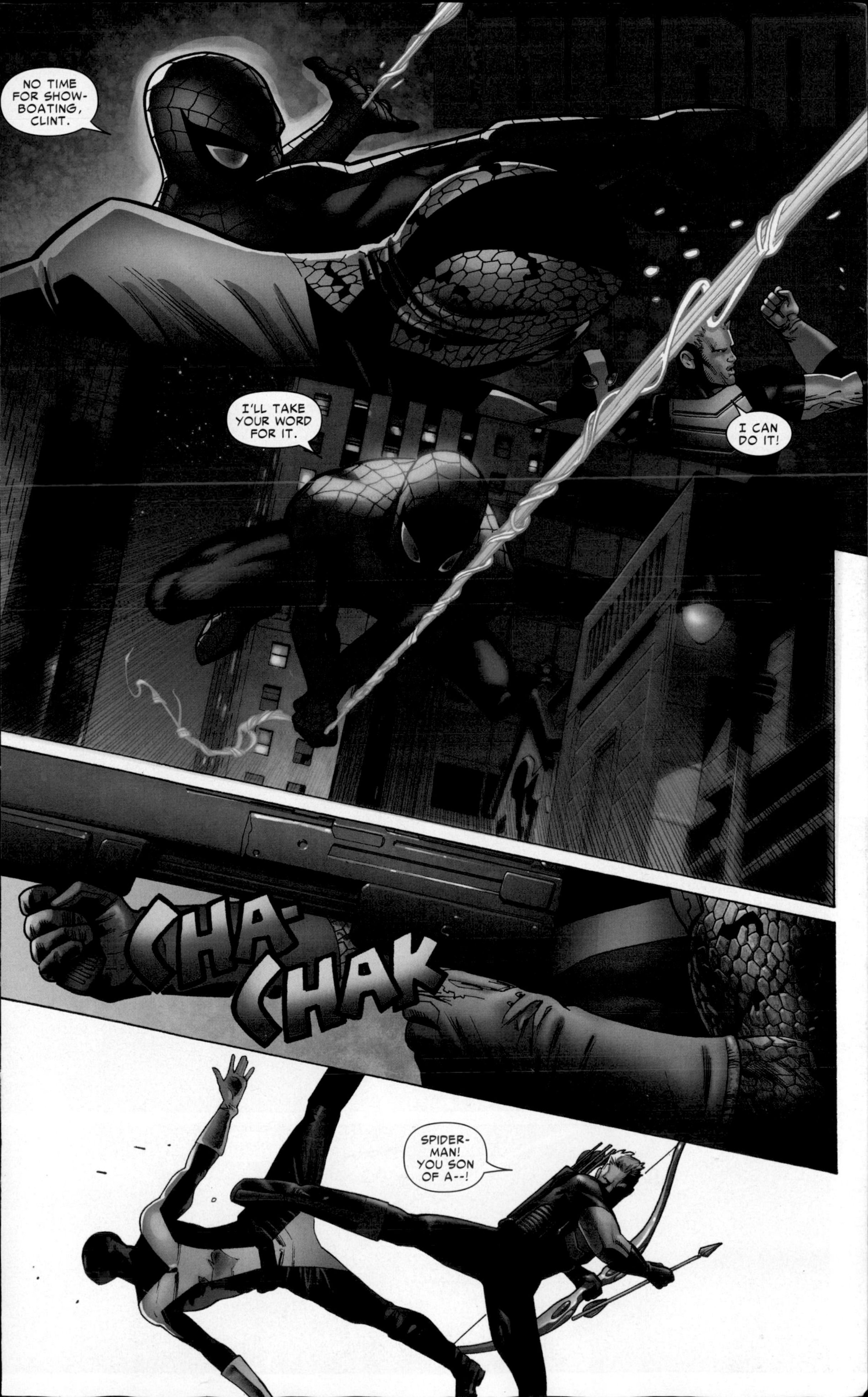
NO TIME FOR SHOW-BOATING, CLINT.
I'LL TAKE YOUR WORD FOR IT.
I CAN DO IT!
CHA-CHAK
SPIDER-MAN! YOU SON OF A--!

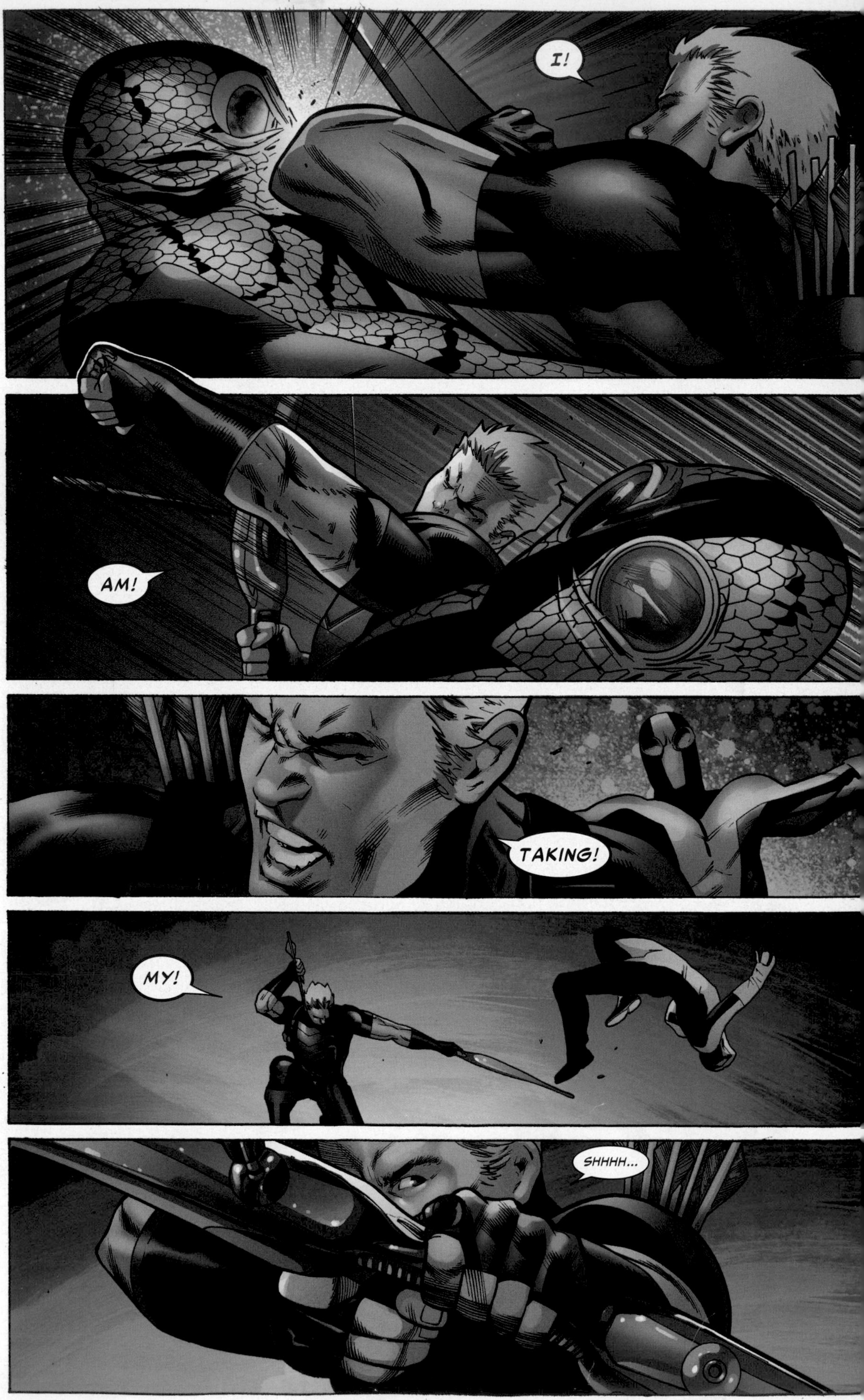
I!
AM!
TAKING!
MY!
SHHHH...

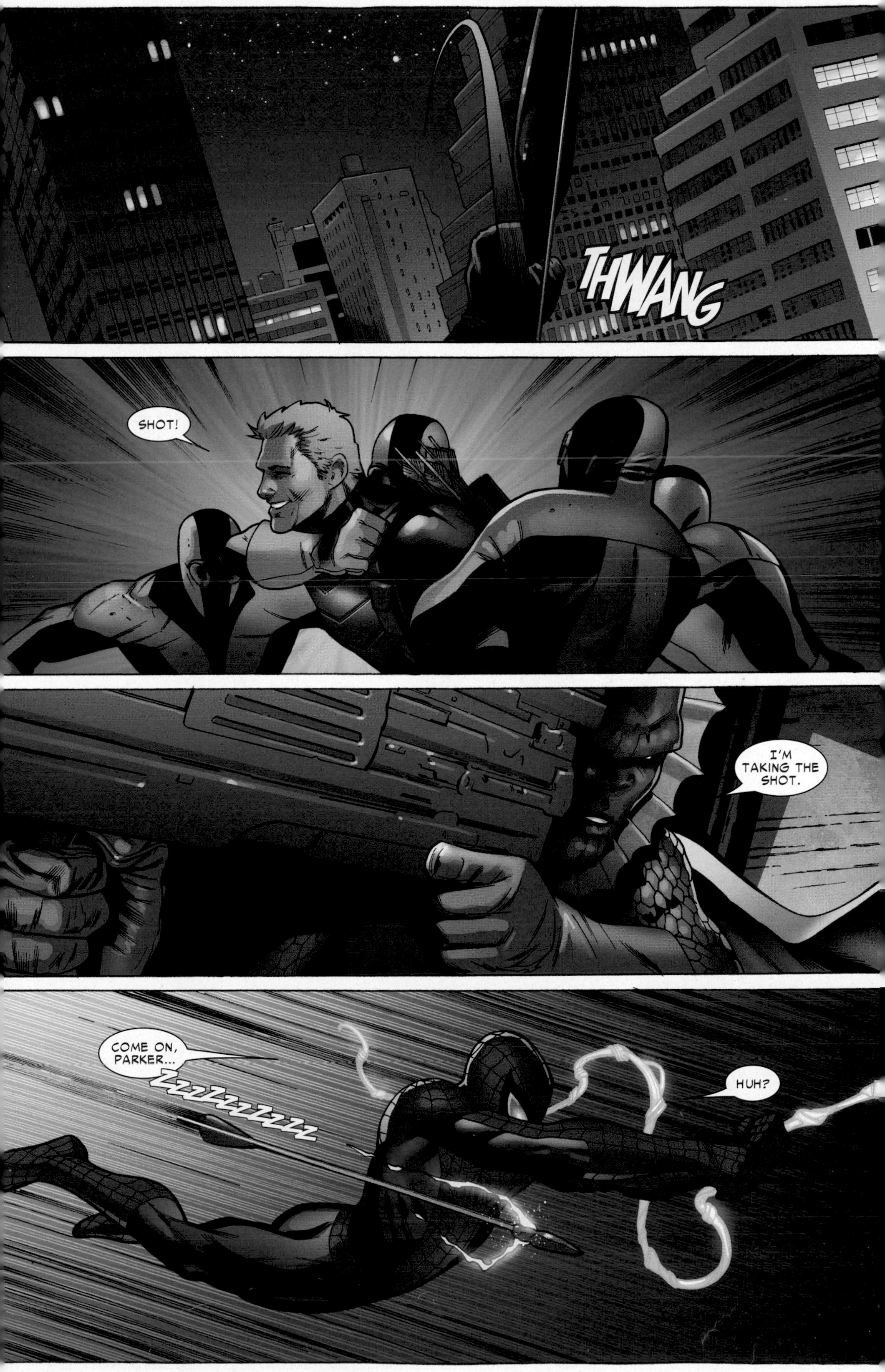
THWANG
SHOT!
I'M TAKING THE SHOT.
COME ON, PARKER...
ZZZZZZZZZZ
HUH?

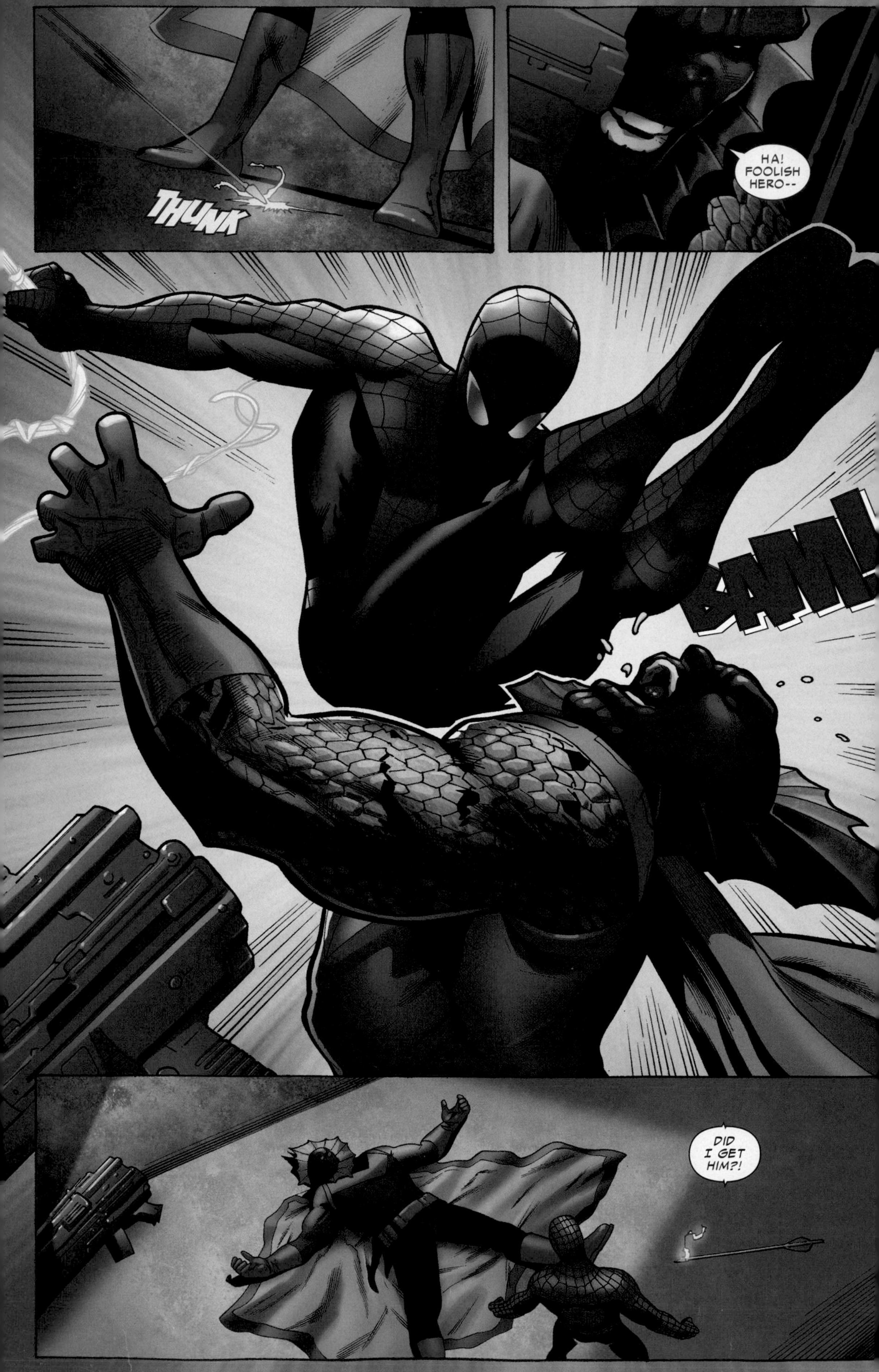
THUNK
HA! FOOLISH HERO--
BAM!
DID I GET HIM?!

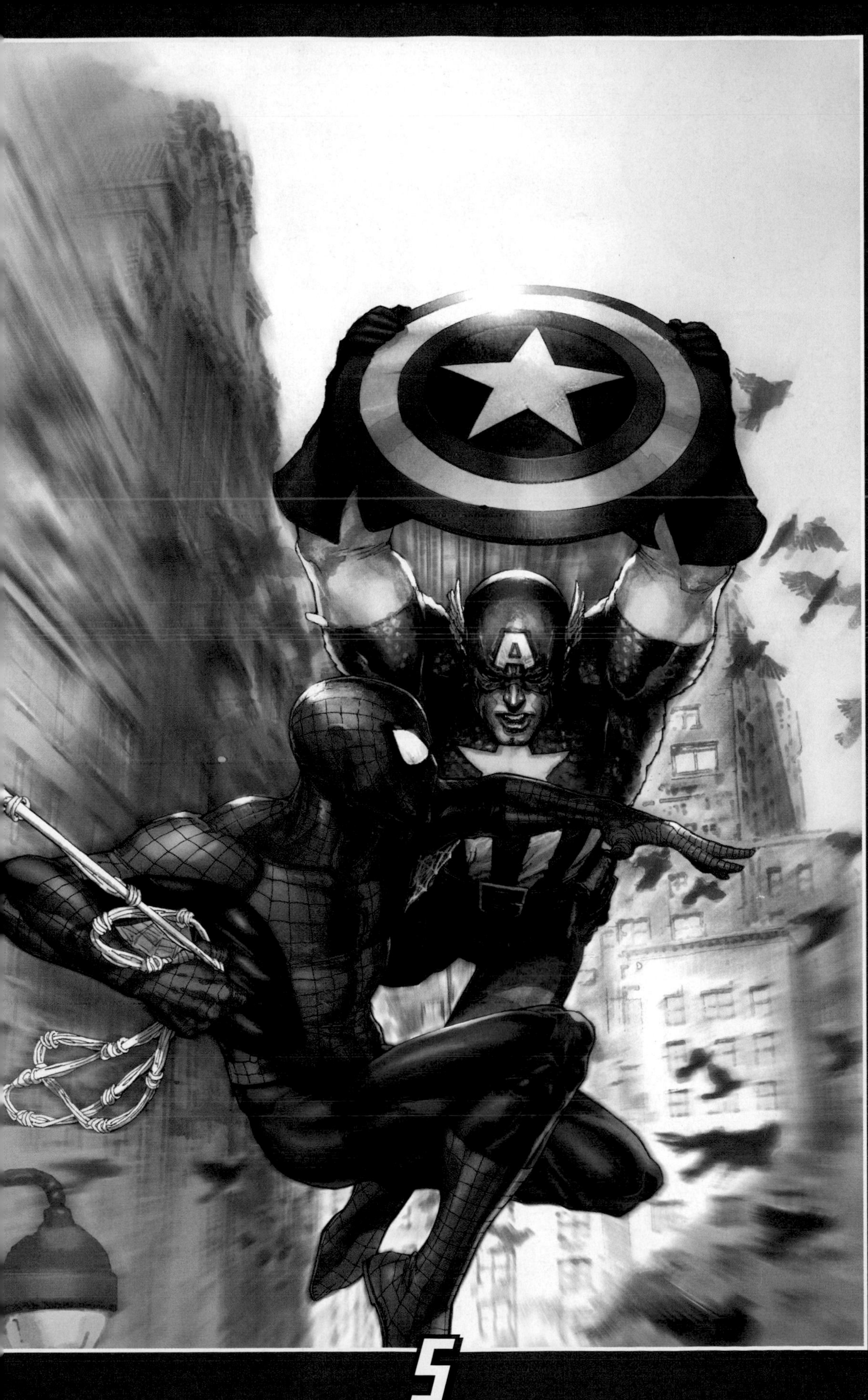

5

While attending a demonstration in radiology, high school student Peter Parker was bitten by a spider which had accidentally been exposed to radioactive rays. Through a miracle of science, Peter soon found that he had gained the spider's powers...and had, in effect become a human spider! Later he joined the Avengers (who have a movie coming out soon). And now he is the...

AVENGING
SPIDER-MAN

Steve Rogers was a frail, Zeb Wells-ish young man who wanted to serve his country during World War II. As part of a Super-Soldier program, he was injected with an experimental serum that enhanced him to the peak of human perfection. Thought to have disappeared during the war, he was later found frozen in the North Atlantic and-- who are we kidding look, you all saw the movie. Indestructible shield etc..etc... He leads the Avengers as--

CAPTAIN
AMERICA

AVENGING
SPIDER-MAN

PREVIOUSLY...

Hawkeye ~~and Spider-Man~~ stopped Sidewinder, of the Serpent Society, *the re* *he* from snake-gassing Grand Central Station. Hawkeye was ~~kind of a jerk~~ but Spider-Man ~~had his back anyway~~. And isn't that what teamwork *didn't wet himself this time* is all about?

WRITER: **ZEB WELLS**   ARTIST: **LEINIL FRANCIS YU**
HAWKEYE   *HAWKEYE*
INKER: ~~**GERRY ALANGUILAN**~~   COLOR ART: ~~**SUNNY GHO**~~
HAWKEYE   *HAWKEYE*
LETTERER: **VC's JOE CARAMAGNA** *HAWKEYE*
HAWKEYE
ASSISTANT EDITOR: ~~**ELLIE PYLE**~~   EDITOR: ~~**STEPHEN WACKER**~~
HAWKEYE   *HAWKEYE*
EXECUTIVE EDITOR: ~~**TOM BREVOORT**~~   EDITOR IN CHIEF: ~~**AXEL ALONSO**~~ *HAWKEYE*
HAWKEYE   *HAWKEYE*
CHIEF CREATIVE OFFICER: ~~**JOE QUESADA**~~   PUBLISHER: ~~**DAN BUCKLEY**~~ EXECUTIVE PRODUCER: **ALAN FINE**

...HAVING COMPLETED HIS PAPER ROUTE IN RECORD TIME, ROGER STEVENS MAKES HIS WAY TO THE LOCAL GOVERNMENT BUILDING TO BUY LIBERTY BONDS WITH HIS PROFITS.

HELLO, SIR! I'D LIKE TO BUY SOME LIBERTY BONDS, PLEASE!

RIGHT AWAY, SON...

BUT HALFWAY THROUGH HIS PATRIOTIC TRANSACTION ROGER NOTICES SOMETHING ISN'T KOSHER!

HEY, THESE LIBERTY BONDS ARE COUNTERFEIT!

YES THEY ARE, YOU PATRIOTIC STOOGE! NO ONE WILL SUPPORT THE WAR EFFORT WHILE I HAVE ANYTHING TO SAY ABOUT IT!

BUT LITTLE DOES THE CONNIVING CLERK KNOW THAT WITH THE TURN OF A PHRASE...

ROCKETS RED GLARE!

...ROGER STEVENS BECOMES SIR SPANGLED, THE HUMAN TANK!

HA! YOU FELL INTO MY TRAP, SIR SPANGLED! ONCE YOU'RE OUT OF THE WAY I'LL SELL ENOUGH PHONY LIBERTY BONDS TO DESTROY AMERICA'S CONFIDENCE!

NOTHING WILL STOP GOOD AMERICANS FROM PURCHASING LIBERTY BONDS!

THESE THUGS ARE IMMUNE TO MY POWERS! (THEY MUST BE COATED IN SALTPETER.) TIME TO CALL IN A LITTLE BACKUP!

LIBERTY BONDS

LIBERTY BONDS! GET 'EM, GIRL!

RUFF

I THINK I'M PICKING UP A SUBTEXT HERE...

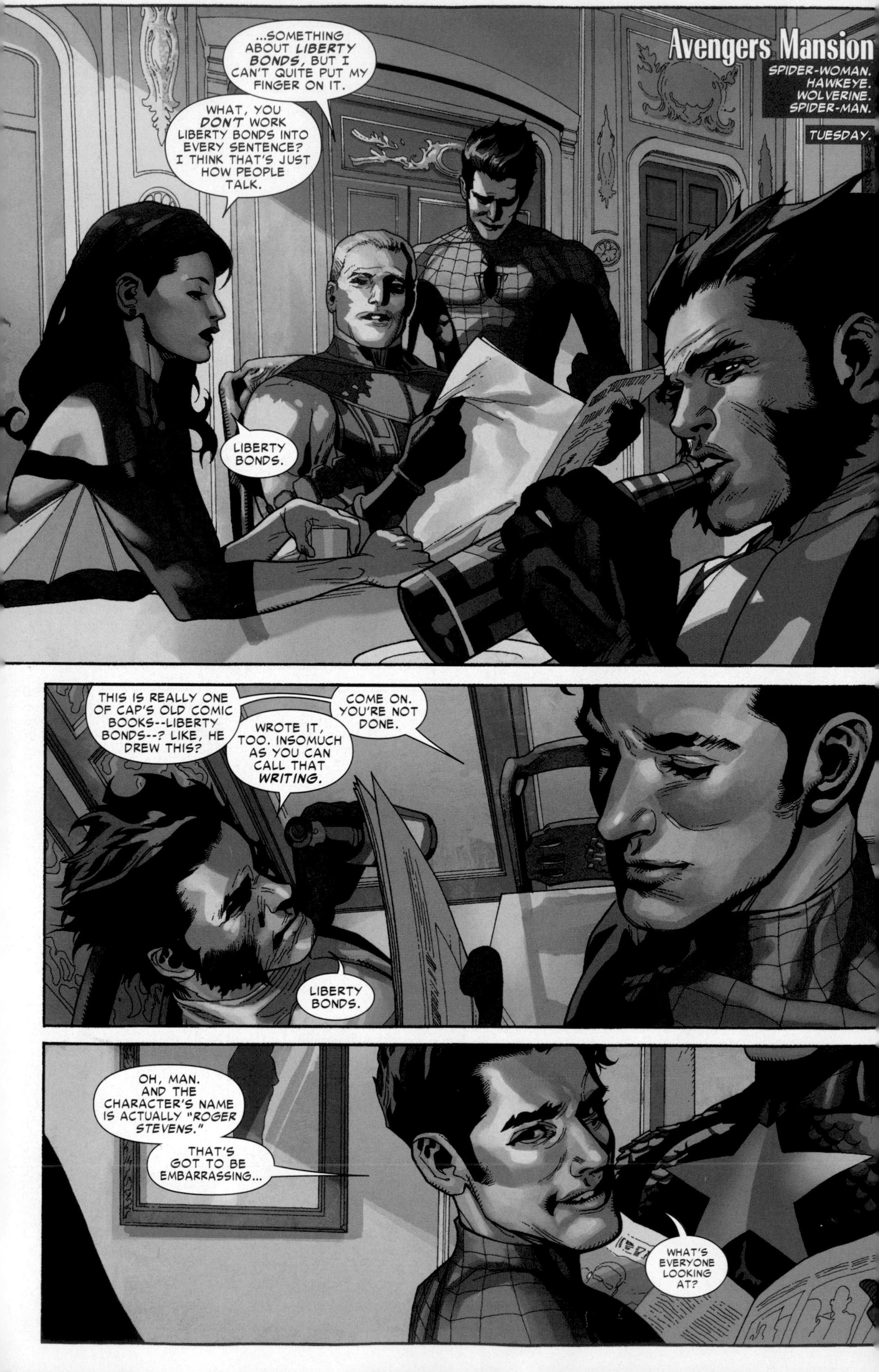
Avengers Mansion
SPIDER-WOMAN. HAWKEYE. WOLVERINE. SPIDER-MAN.
TUESDAY.
...SOMETHING ABOUT LIBERTY BONDS, BUT I CAN'T QUITE PUT MY FINGER ON IT.
WHAT, YOU DON'T WORK LIBERTY BONDS INTO EVERY SENTENCE? I THINK THAT'S JUST HOW PEOPLE TALK.
LIBERTY BONDS.
THIS IS REALLY ONE OF CAP'S OLD COMIC BOOKS--LIBERTY BONDS--? LIKE, HE DREW THIS?
WROTE IT, TOO. INSOMUCH AS YOU CAN CALL THAT WRITING.
COME ON. YOU'RE NOT DONE.
LIBERTY BONDS.
OH, MAN. AND THE CHARACTER'S NAME IS ACTUALLY "ROGER STEVENS."
THAT'S GOT TO BE EMBARRASSING...
WHAT'S EVERYONE LOOKING AT?

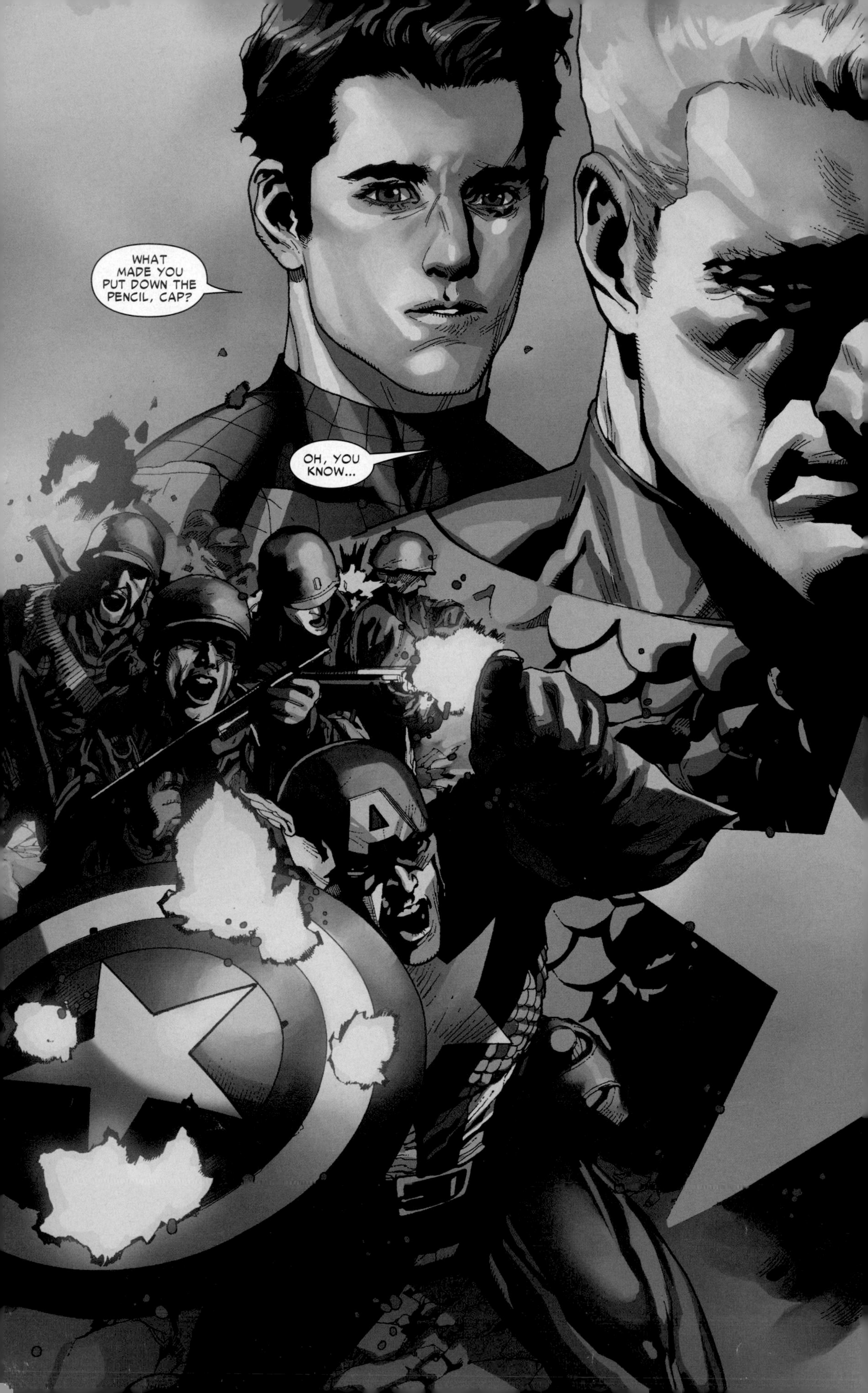
WHAT MADE YOU PUT DOWN THE PENCIL, CAP?
OH, YOU KNOW...

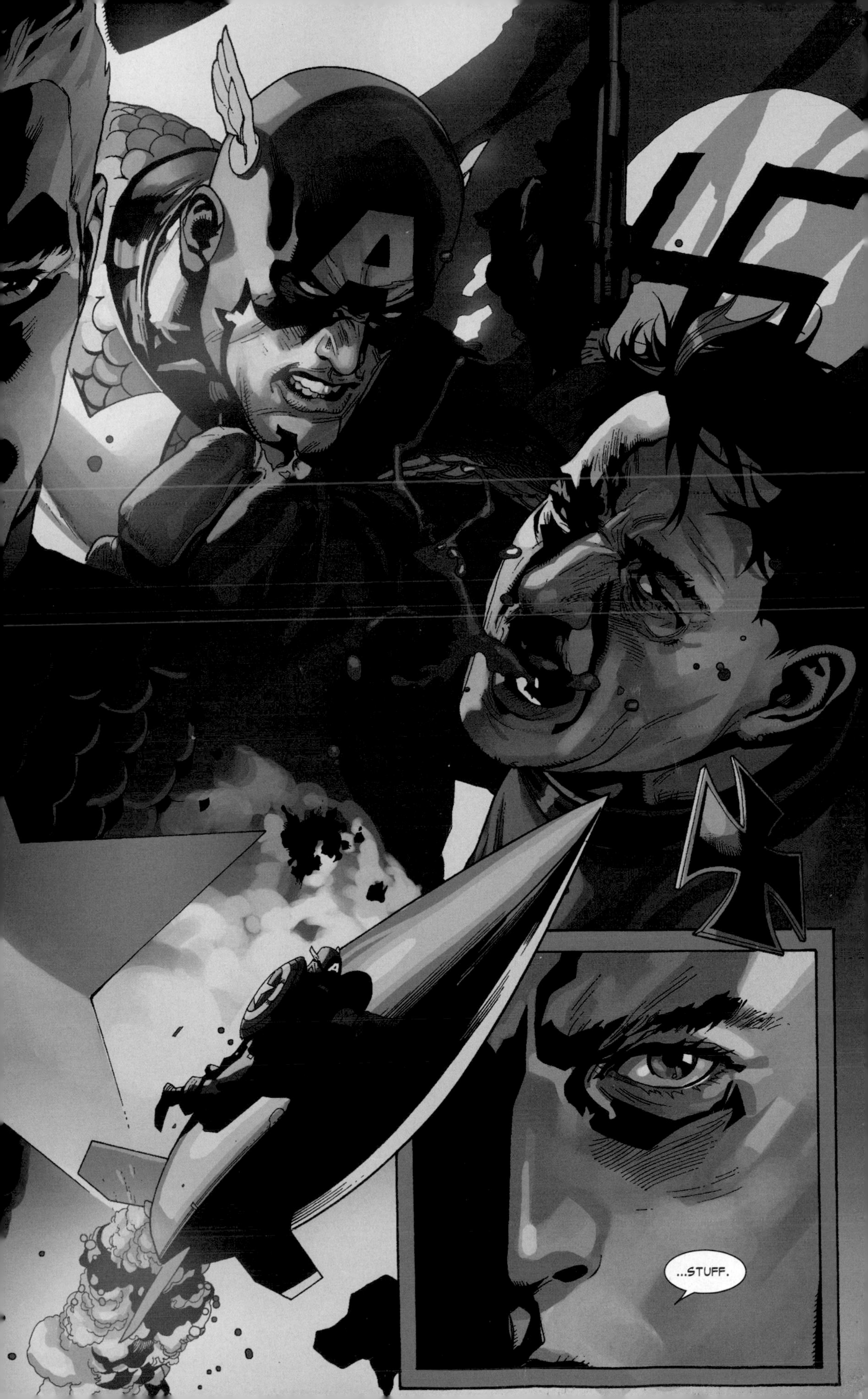
...STUFF.

BUT ENOUGH OF THAT. *AVENGERS.* WE'VE GOT WORK TO DO. I'LL GET HULK AND MEET YOU IN THE MINIQUIN.

HEY, CAP. I THOUGHT YOUR COMIC WAS REALLY NEAT. WE WERE JUST HAVING FUN BACK THERE.

DON'T THINK TWICE ABOUT IT, SPIDER-MAN. IT'S ALL IN THE PAST.

HMMM...

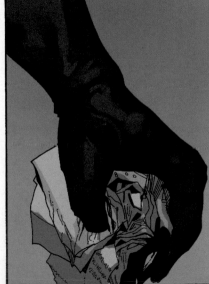

HE...

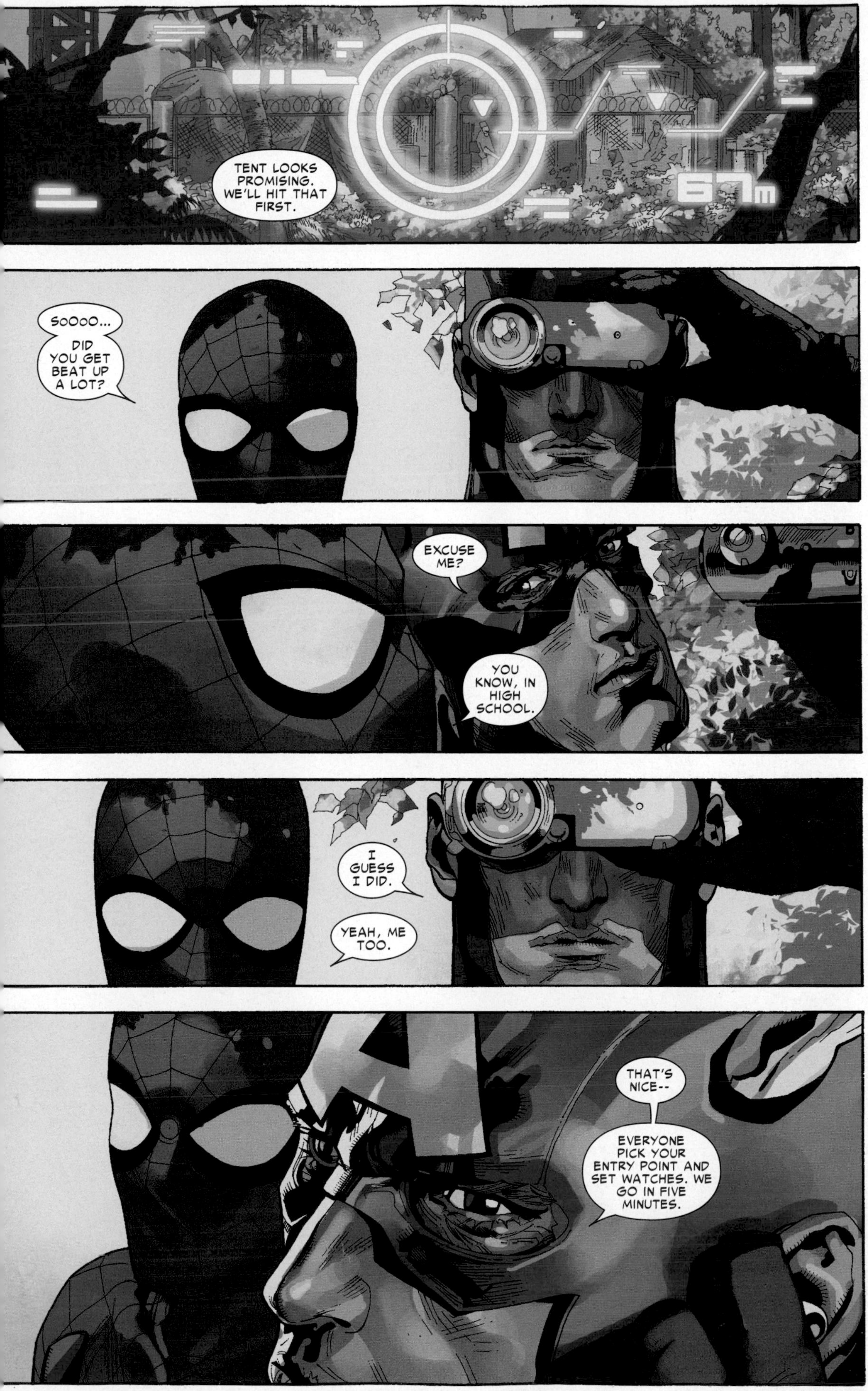
TENT LOOKS PROMISING. WE'LL HIT THAT FIRST.
67m
SOOOO... DID YOU GET BEAT UP A LOT?
EXCUSE ME?
YOU KNOW, IN HIGH SCHOOL.
I GUESS I DID.
YEAH, ME TOO.
THAT'S NICE--
EVERYONE PICK YOUR ENTRY POINT AND SET WATCHES. WE GO IN FIVE MINUTES.

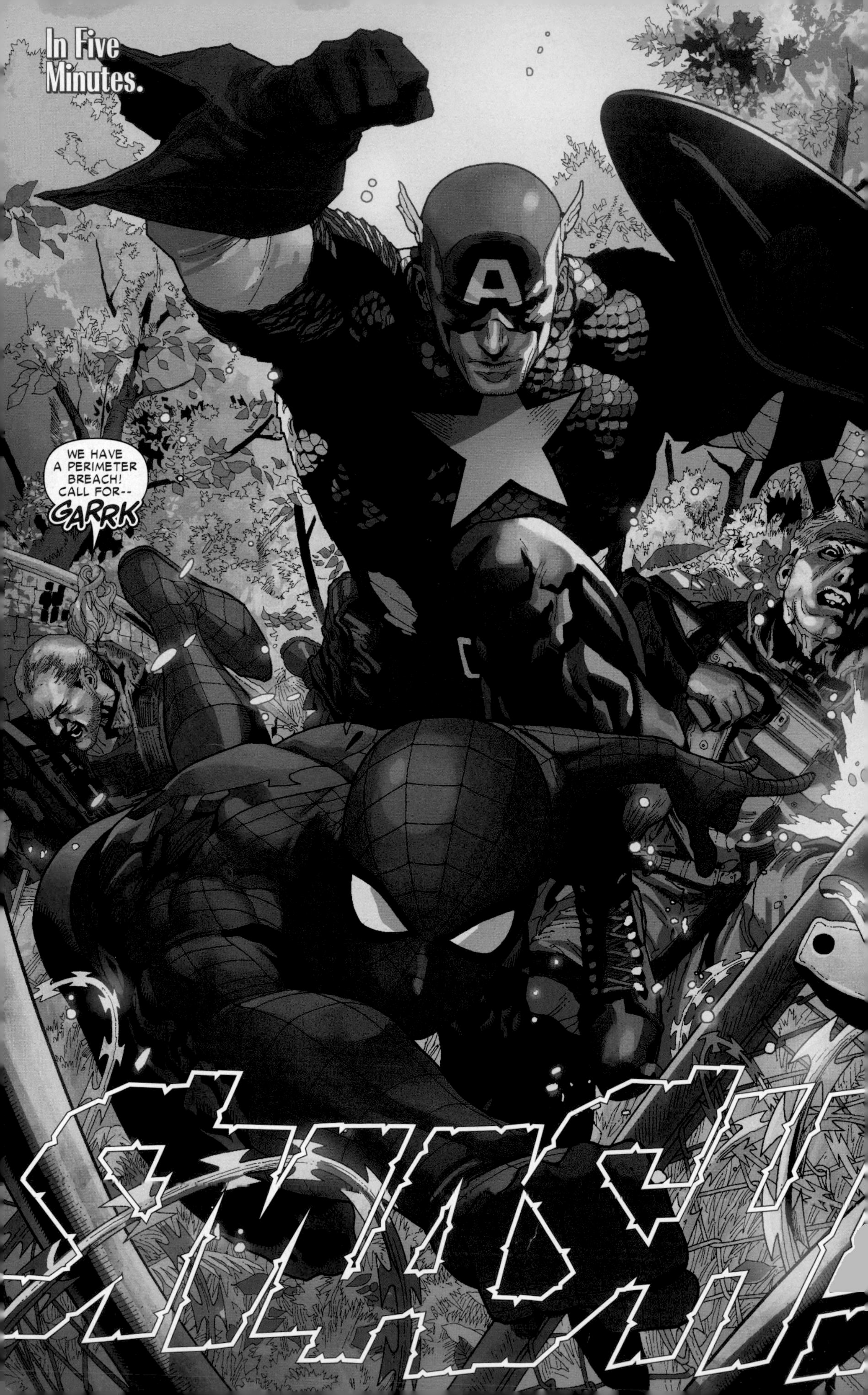
In Five Minutes.
WE HAVE A PERIMETER BREACH! CALL FOR-- GARRK

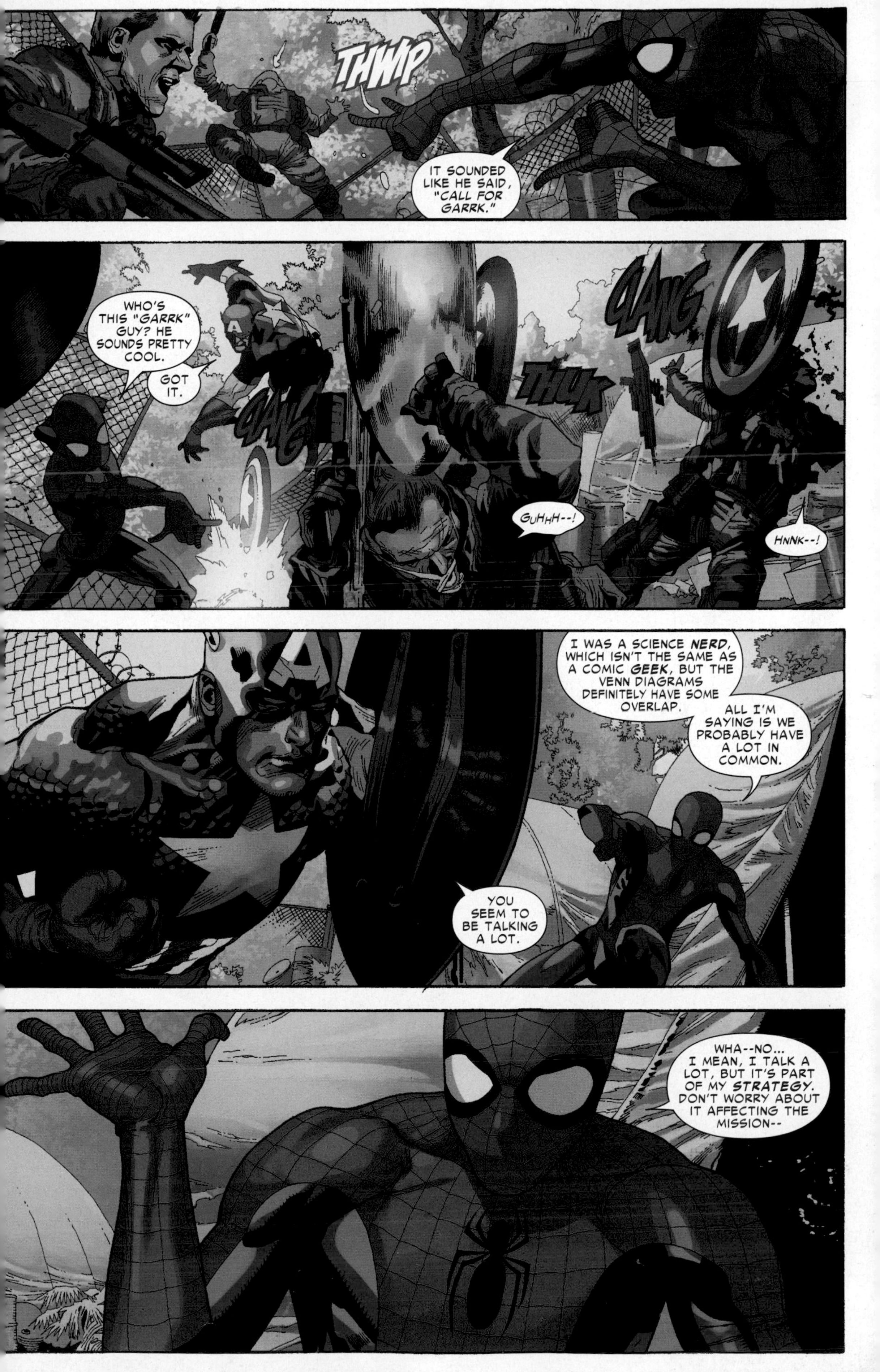
THWMP
IT SOUNDED LIKE HE SAID, "CALL FOR GARRK."
WHO'S THIS "GARRK" GUY? HE SOUNDS PRETTY COOL.
GOT IT.
CLANG
CLANG
THUK
GUHHH--!
HNNK--!
I WAS A SCIENCE NERD, WHICH ISN'T THE SAME AS A COMIC GEEK, BUT THE VENN DIAGRAMS DEFINITELY HAVE SOME OVERLAP.
ALL I'M SAYING IS WE PROBABLY HAVE A LOT IN COMMON.
YOU SEEM TO BE TALKING A LOT.
WHA--NO... I MEAN, I TALK A LOT, BUT IT'S PART OF MY STRATEGY. DON'T WORRY ABOUT IT AFFECTING THE MISSION--

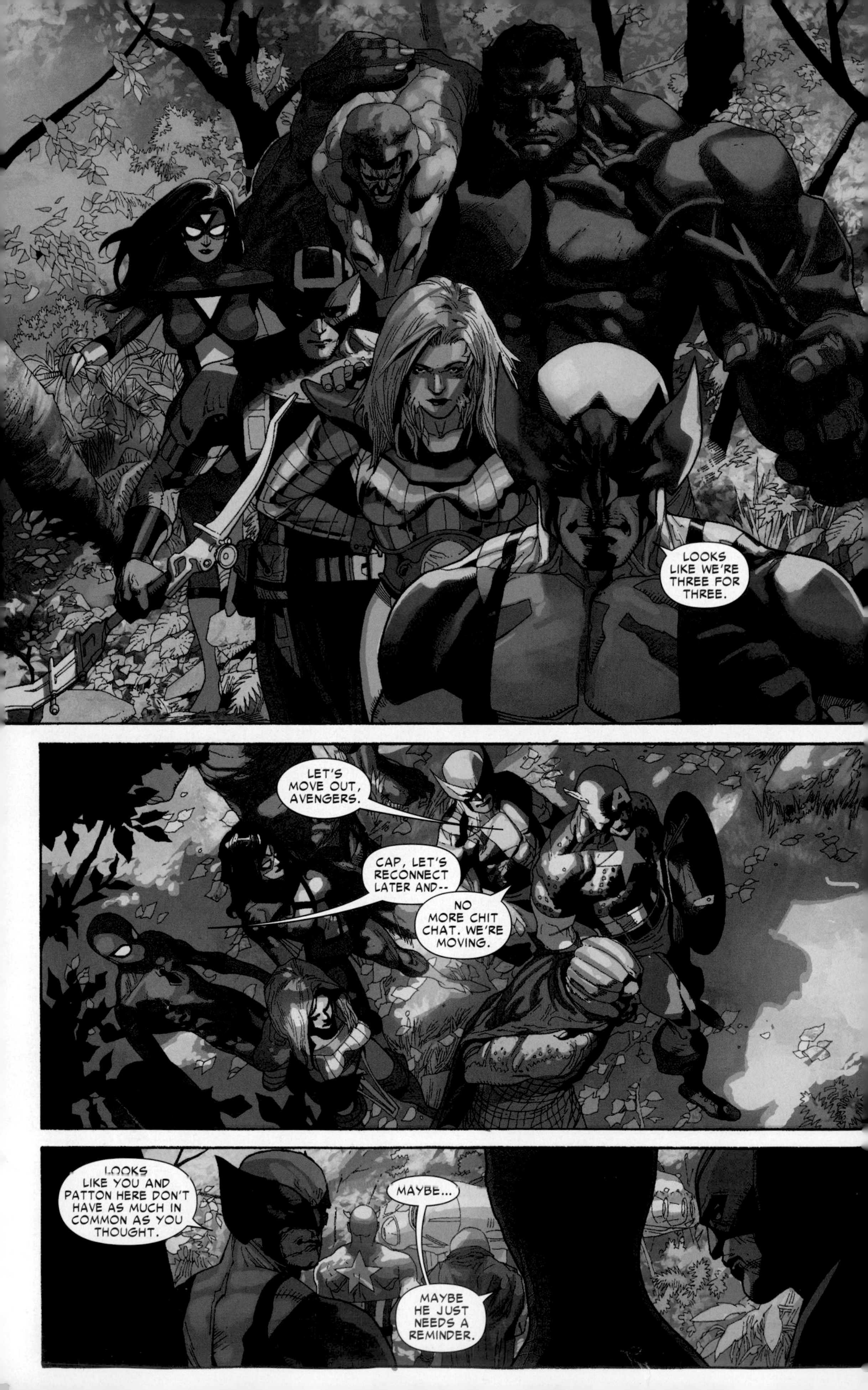
LOOKS LIKE WE'RE THREE FOR THREE.
LET'S MOVE OUT, AVENGERS.
CAP, LET'S RECONNECT LATER AND--
NO MORE CHIT CHAT. WE'RE MOVING.
LOOKS LIKE YOU AND PATTON HERE DON'T HAVE AS MUCH IN COMMON AS YOU THOUGHT.
MAYBE...
MAYBE HE JUST NEEDS A REMINDER.

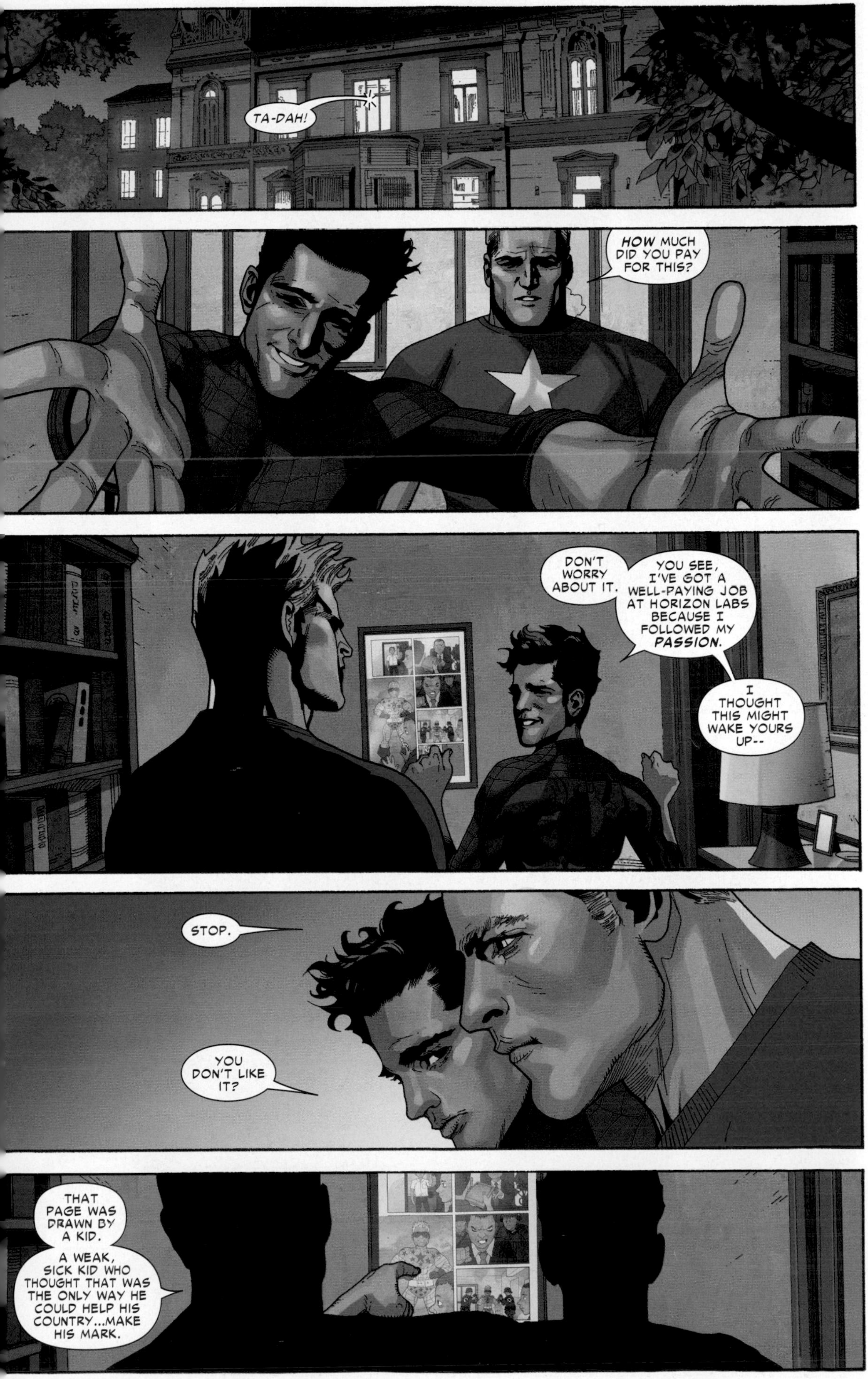
TA-DAH!
HOW MUCH DID YOU PAY FOR THIS?
DON'T WORRY ABOUT IT.
YOU SEE, I'VE GOT A WELL-PAYING JOB AT HORIZON LABS BECAUSE I FOLLOWED MY PASSION.
I THOUGHT THIS MIGHT WAKE YOURS UP--
STOP.
YOU DON'T LIKE IT?
THAT PAGE WAS DRAWN BY A KID.
A WEAK, SICK KID WHO THOUGHT THAT WAS THE ONLY WAY HE COULD HELP HIS COUNTRY...MAKE HIS MARK.

I WAS JUST THROWING THIS STUFF OUT. WASN'T GOING TO PLAY WITH IT, I SWEAR.

IF THIS IS A SURPRISE INSPECTION OF MY ROOM, I'LL TELL YOU RIGHT NOW, I'M NOT GOING TO PASS. IT'S A...UHHH...KANG-RELATED MESS.

AND THAT SMELL ISN'T ME. TRUTH IS, I THINK WOLVERINE PEED IN HERE SOME-WHERES.

SO WHAT'D YA THINK OF THE BACHELOR? PRETTY CRAZY, HUH?

SAY WHAT NOW?

ACTUALLY, I NEED YOUR HELP...

THOUGHT A LOT ABOUT WHAT YOU SAID...DECIDED TO DO SOME DOODLING. SEE IF I COULD CREATE A SUPER HERO THAT WASN'T AN INSENSITIVE IDIOT.

COULDN'T CRACK IT, THOUGH. I NEEDED SOME HELP.

BUT YOU WEREN'T IN THE KITCHEN TO BRAINSTORM LIKE YOU SAID YOU'D BE...

OH, RIGHT. HEH.

WOW, WHAT A JERK I WAS.

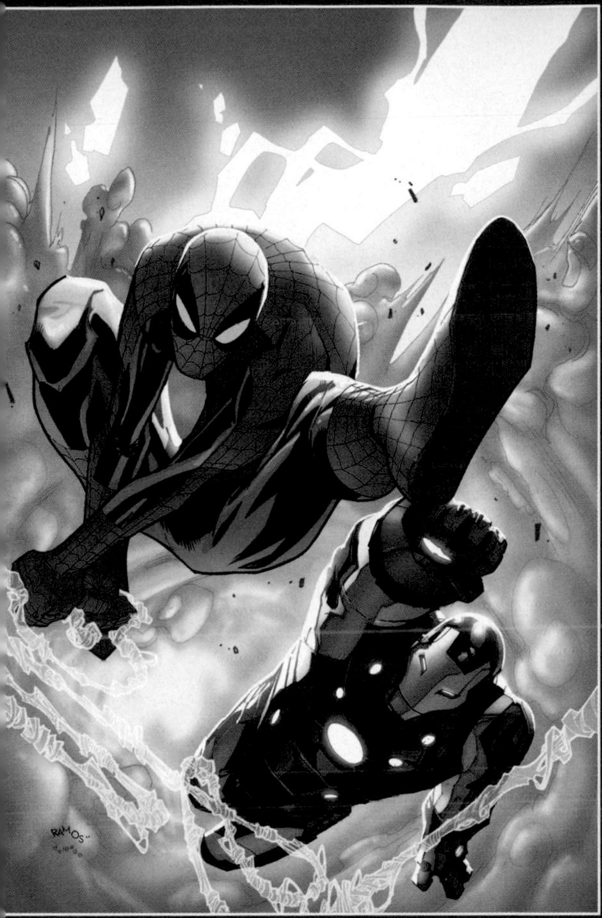
RAMOS

#1 VARIANT BY
HUMBERTO RAMOS & EDGAR DELGADO

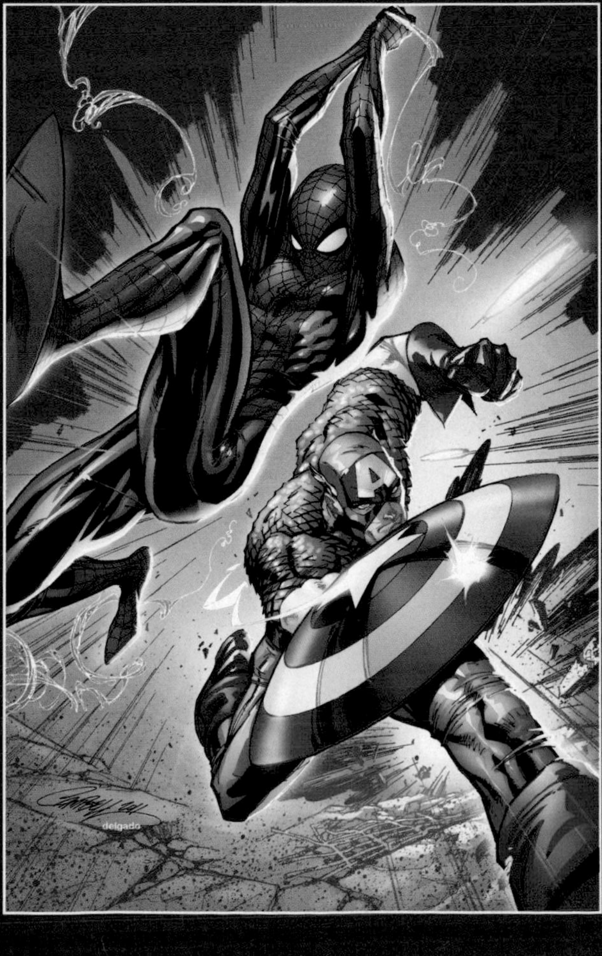
delgado

#1 VARIANT BY
J. SCOTT CAMPBELL & EDGAR DELGADO

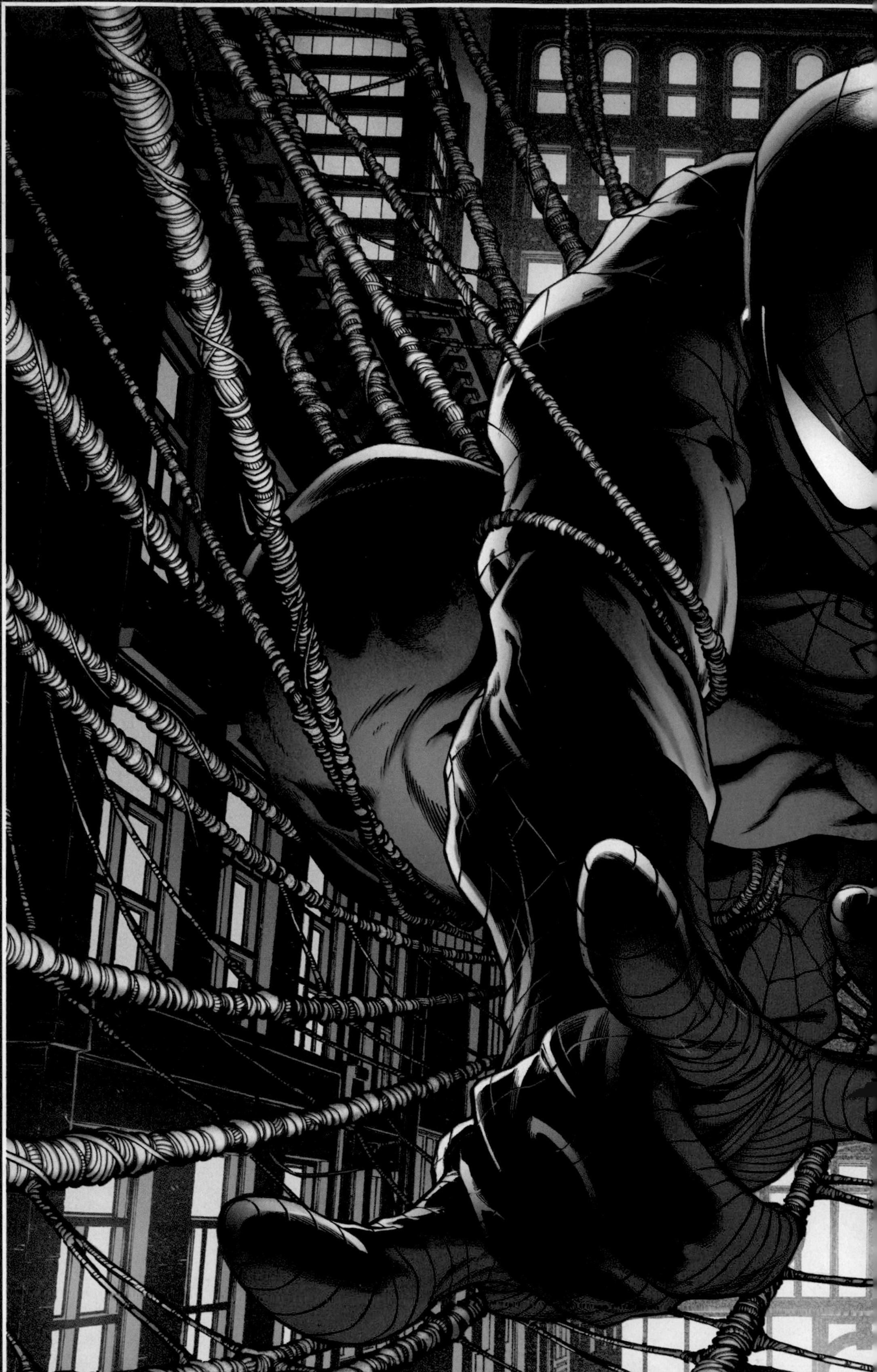

#1 VARIANT BY **JOE QUESADA, DANNY MIKI & RICHARD ISANOVE**

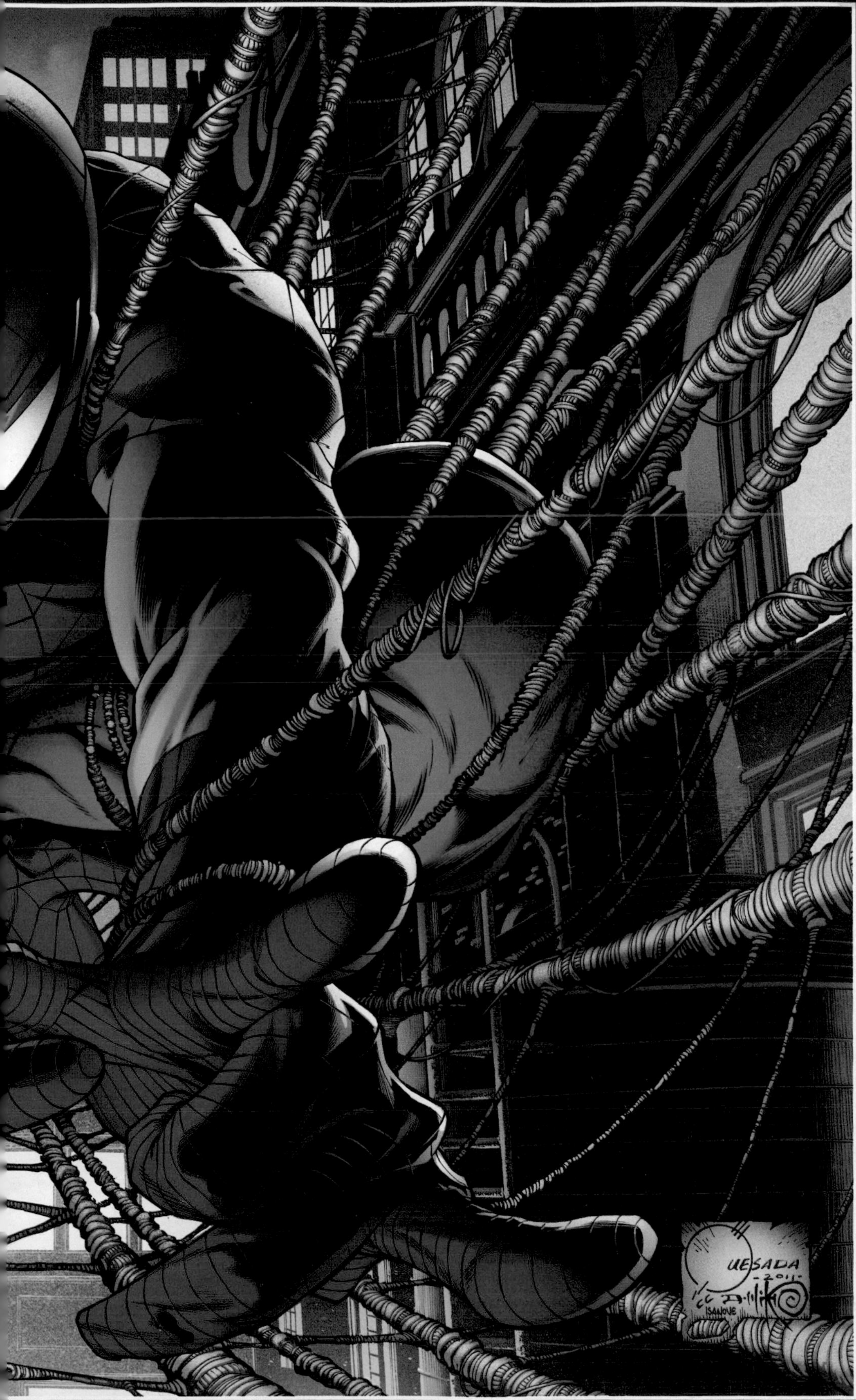
UESADA
-2011-
ISANOVE

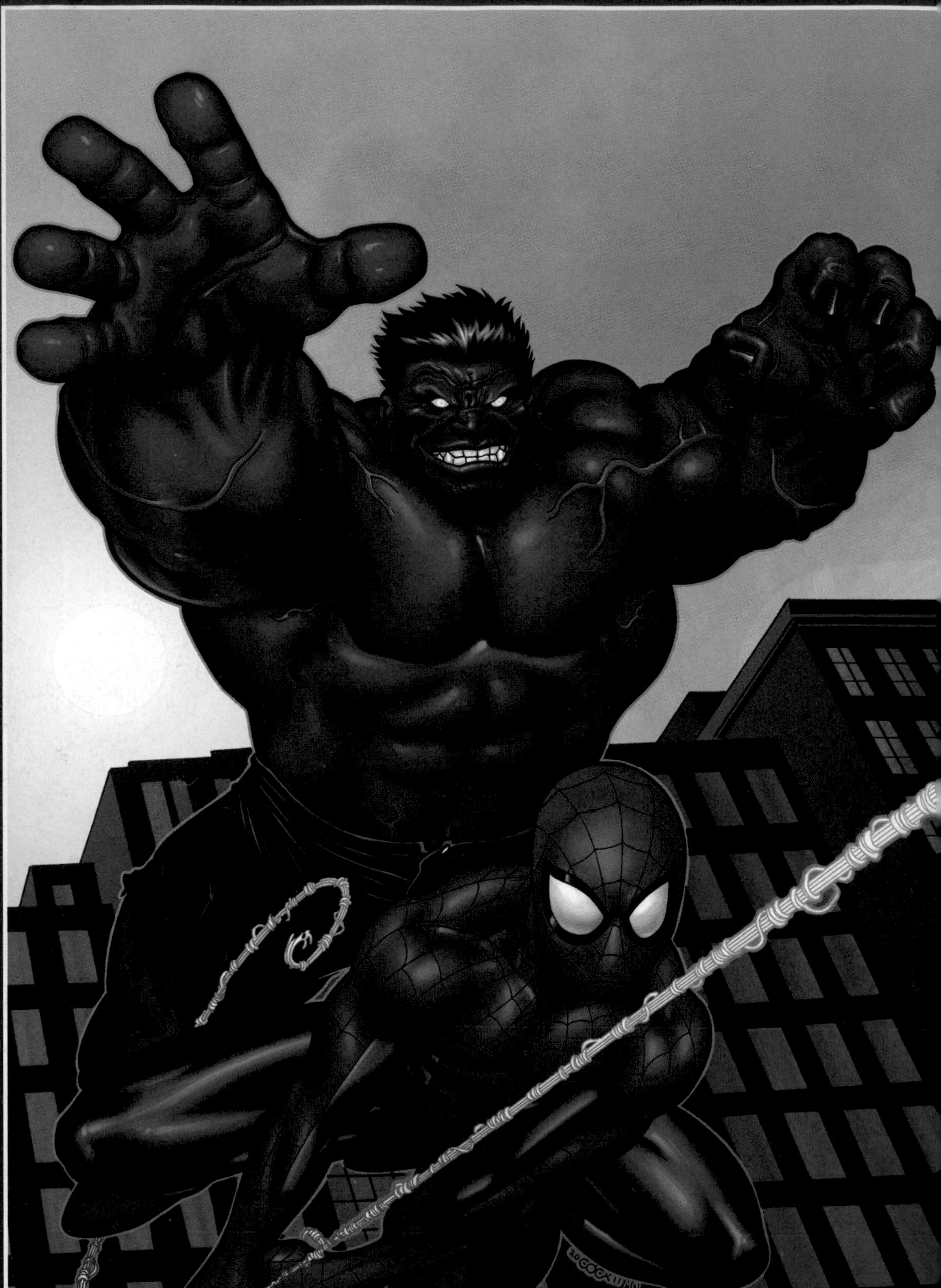

#2 VARIANT BY **ED McGUINNESS, DEXTER VINES & MORRY HOLLOWELL**

3 SPIDER-MAN 50TH ANNIVERSARY VARIANT BY **HUMBERTO RAMOS & EDGAR DELGADO**

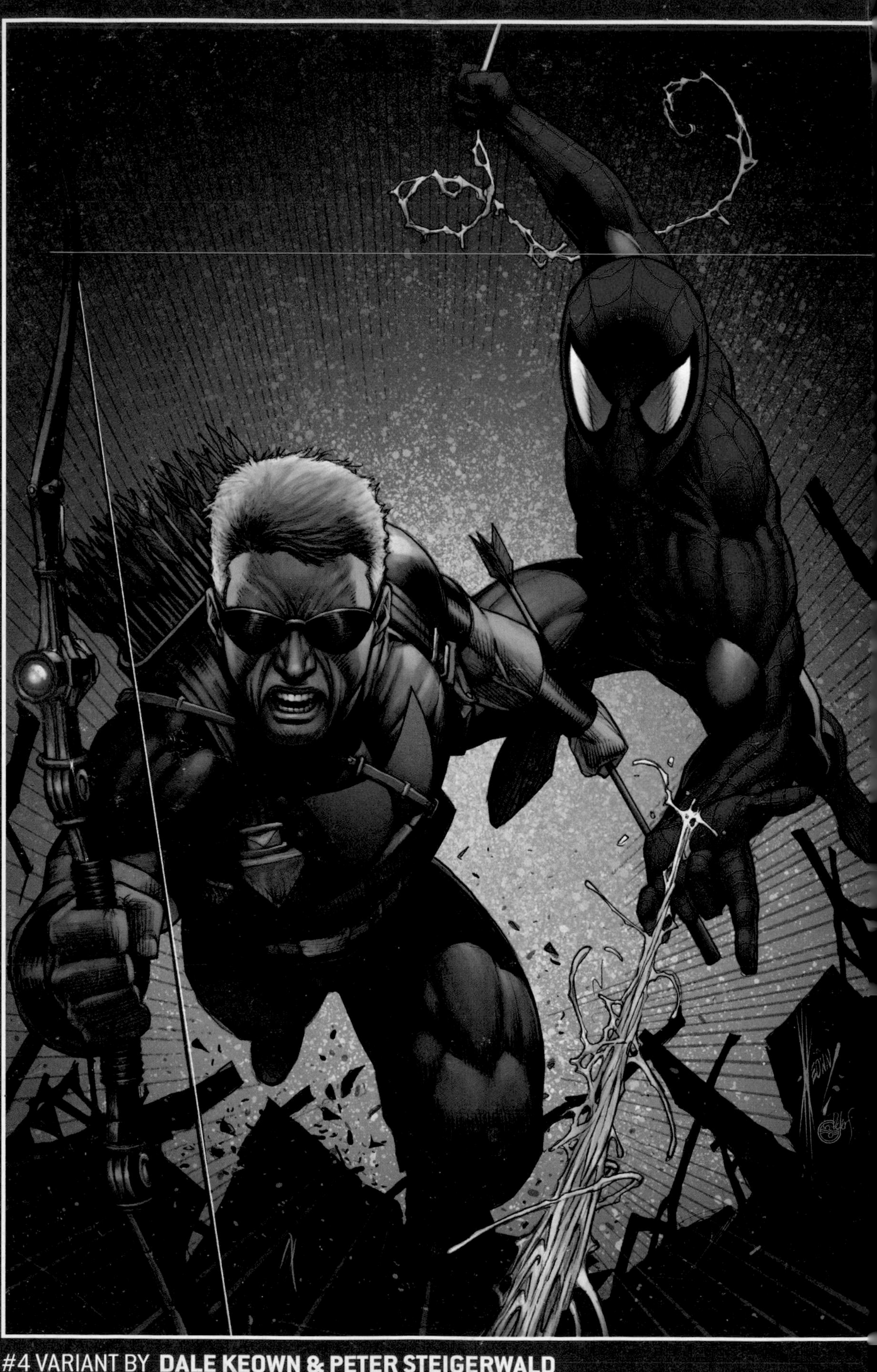

#4 VARIANT BY **DALE KEOWN & PETER STEIGERWALD**